Hidden

BELGIUM

DEREK BLYTH

INTRODUCTION

HIDDEN BELGIUM is an alternative guidebook that aims to inspire you with stories of more than 300 curious and unexpected places to visit. It takes you off the beaten track to look at sites most people don't know about, such as the tiny Belgian village where Hitler commanded the invasion of France, the ghost railway stations of Brussels and the eccentric grotto in an Ardennes village dedicated to the patron saint of lost things. The aim is to awaken your senses, revive your curiosity and take you to places with a story to tell. You might be inspired to visit a small town that was once an independent country, wander through a garden dedicated to unpleasant smells, or eat lunch in a former science lab.
Some people argue that Belgium is a boring country, but this book sets out to prove that it is in fact one of the most interesting countries in Europe. It has a rich history, a stunning range of architectural styles and some fabulous places to spend a night.

The book doesn't cover everything there is to see in Belgium. You can find out about the popular places by dropping into a tourist office or reading through some Belgian blogs. The aim of *Hidden Belgium* is to tempt you to go a bit beyond the ordinary and explore places most people don't know about. Some of these destinations can admittedly be a little frustrating to visit. They might be difficult to find, or they might only be open a few days a month. You might arrive to find a place has closed, or disappeared entirely. You sometimes need to be patient, but you will eventually come across something astonishing.

This is meant to be a book to pick up for inspiration on a rainy afternoon. It is meant for adventurous travellers, urban explorers and anyone who believes the world is still full of curious and forgotten places waiting to be discovered.

ABOUT THE AUTHOR

DEREK BLYTH has lived in Belgium for more than 30 years. Working as a journalist, he knows the country intimately and has explored almost every corner, from the small beach towns on the North Sea to the sleepy villages deep in the Ardennes. Formerly editor-in-chief of *The Bulletin* magazine, he has written countless articles and several books on Belgium, including the bestselling *The 500 Hidden Secrets of Bruges, Brussels, Ghent* and *Antwerp*. He also organises walking tours and lectures in Brussels, Antwerp and Ghent.

The author could not have written this book on his own. He would like to thank all the people who have provided tips and suggestions over the years, including countless Belgians he has met in the street who have taken the time to share a story or point out an obscure detail.

Particular thanks must go to the editorial team at Luster, who have generously shared details of their favourite spots. He would also like to thank Mary Maclure who has been an enthusiastic companion on trips that sometimes ended up in peculiar places.

HOW TO USE THIS BOOK

The idea behind this book is to list places the author would recommend to a friend who was looking for a surprising destination or an unusual experience. It is different from other guidebooks in listing places by category rather than location. But the maps allow you to put together a journey linking several hidden places.

Most of the destinations mentioned in the book can be reached by train, bike or on foot. But occasionally a car is needed to get to the more remote spots. The author advises using trains where possible. Tickets are reasonably cheap in Belgium, especially at weekends, when you can buy half price fares across the entire country. You can also obtain special 10-journey tickets that make train travel affordable.

The author would also encourage the use of bicycles to get around. The cycling organisations in Flanders and Wallonia have developed a network of cycle routes based on numbered waypoints. This makes it simple to plan routes along quiet canal towpaths or abandoned railway lines.

But possibly the best way of getting around is on foot, especially in old Belgian cities dating back to the early Middle Ages. They were originally made to be explored at the human pace of three kilometres an hour. So pack an umbrella, turn off your phone and set off on a micro adventure. Only then will you discover the strange and inspiring places that are almost unknown.

DISCOVER MORE ONLINE

Hidden Belgium is part of the internationally successful travel guide series called *The 500 Hidden Secrets*. The series covers over 40 destinations and includes city guides, regional guides and guides that focus on a specific theme.

Curious about the other destinations? Or looking for inspiration for your next city trip? Visit THE500HIDDENSECRETS.COM. Here you can order every guide from our online shop and find tons of interesting travel content.

Also, don't forget to follow us on Instagram or Facebook for dreamy travel photos and ideas, as well as up-to-date information. Our socials are the easiest way to get in touch with us: we love hearing from you and appreciate all feedback.

the500hiddensecrets

@500hiddensecrets #500hiddensecrets

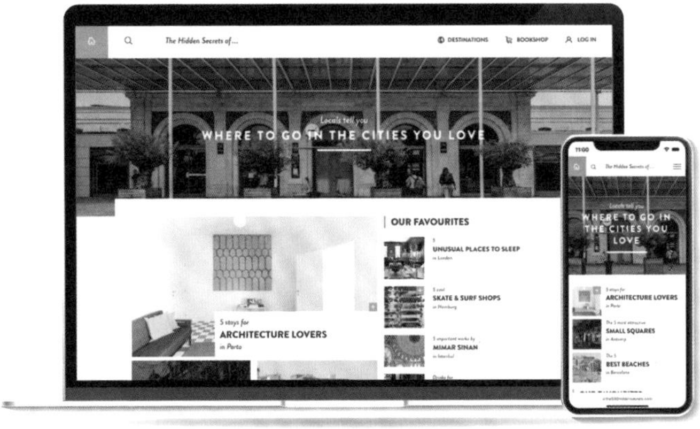

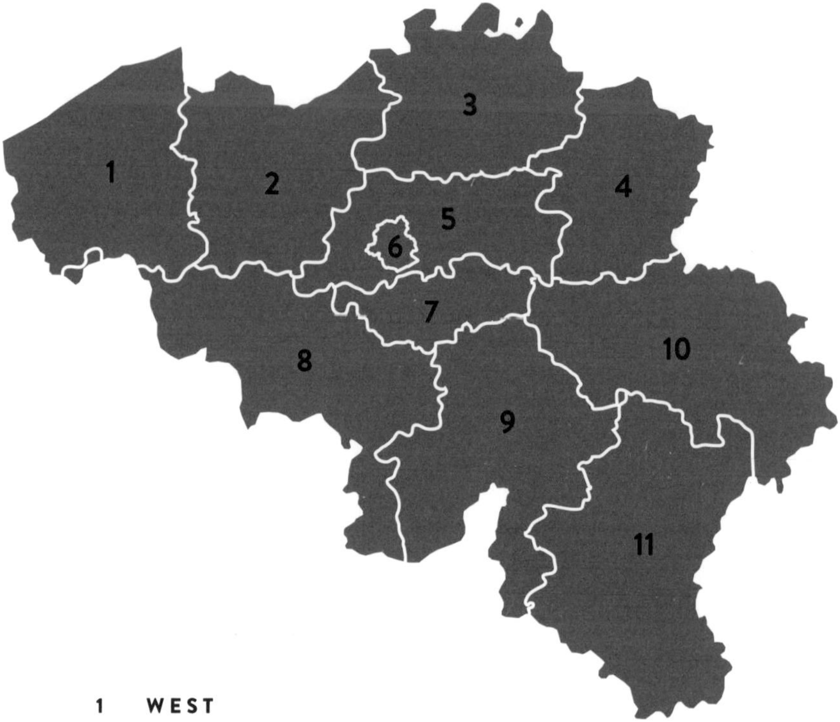

1 WEST FLANDERS

2 EAST FLANDERS

3 ANTWERP

4 LIMBURG

5 FLEMISH BRABANT

6 BRUSSELS

7 WALLOON BRABANT

8 HAINAUT

9 NAMUR

10 LIÈGE

11 LUXEMBOURG

1 WEST FLANDERS

Knokke
Zeebrugge
Blankenberge
De Haan
Ostend
Coast
Bruges
Oostduinkerke
Koksijde
Diksmuide
Langemark
Zonnebeke
Poperinge
Ypres
Voormezele
Zillebeke
Harelbeke
Kortrijk
De Klijte
Kemmel
Heuvelland

2 EAST FLANDERS

3 ANTWERP

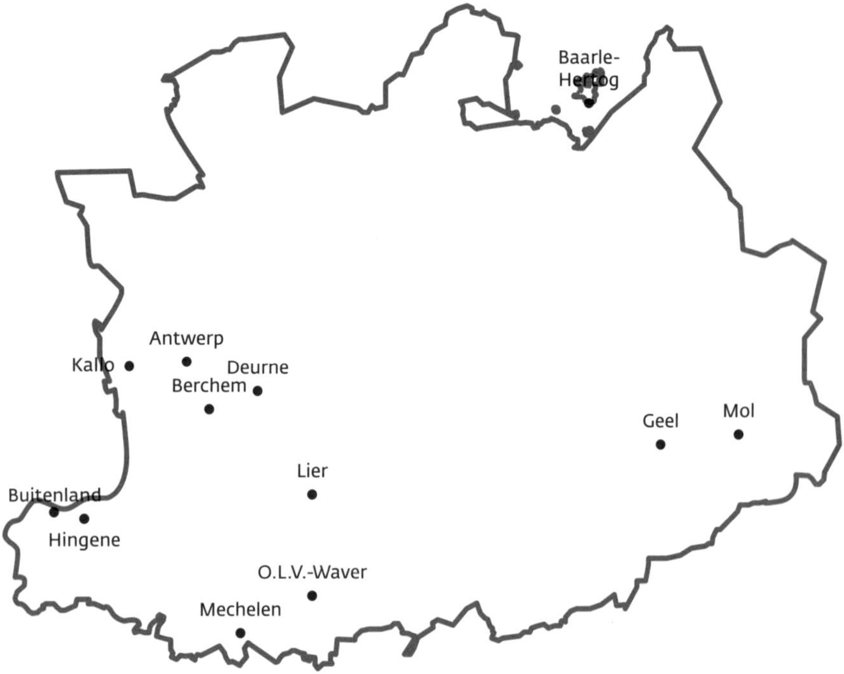
Baarle-
Hertog
Antwerp
Kallo
Deurne
Berchem
Geel
Mol
Lier
Buitenland
Hingene
O.L.V.-Waver
Mechelen

4 LIMBURG

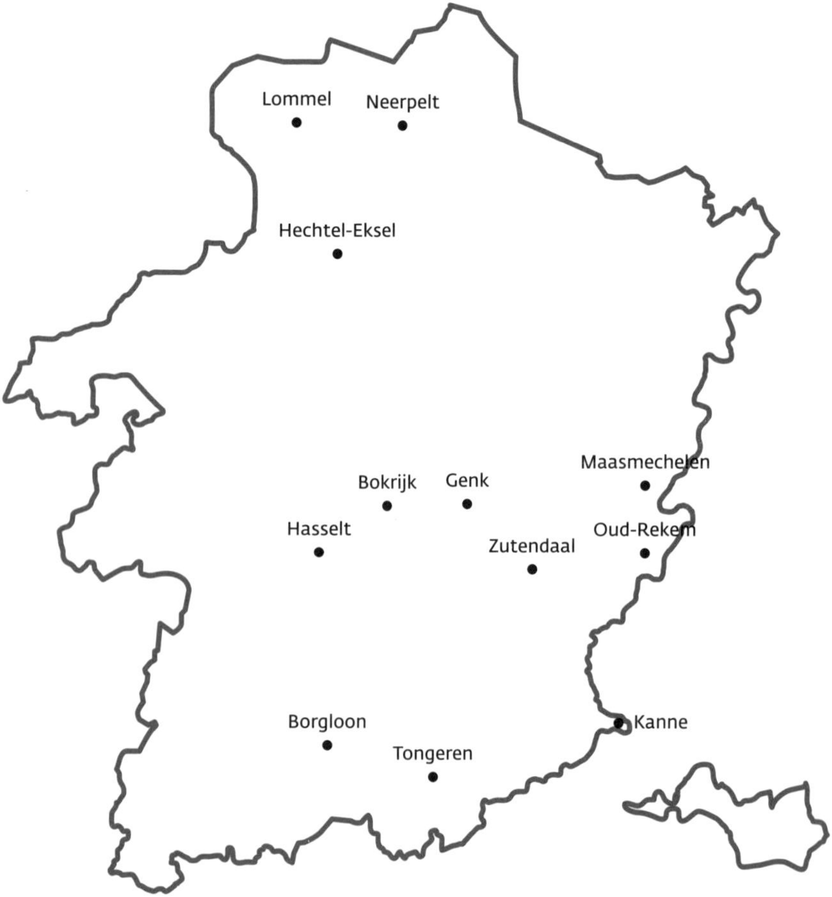

Lommel
Neerpelt
Hechtel-Eksel
Maasmechelen
Bokrijk
Genk
Hasselt
Zutendaal
Oud-Rekem
Borgloon
Kanne
Tongeren

5 FLEMISH BRABANT

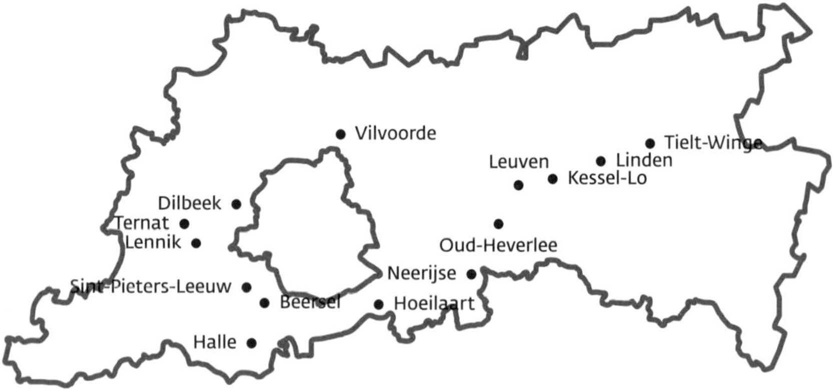

6 BRUSSELS

1020
Laeken
1090
Jette
1030
Schaerbeek
1000
Brussels
1200
Woluwe-
Saint-
Lambert
1048
European Quarter
1050
Ixelles
1040
Etterbeek
1060
Saint-Gilles
1180
Uccle

7 WALLOON BRABANT

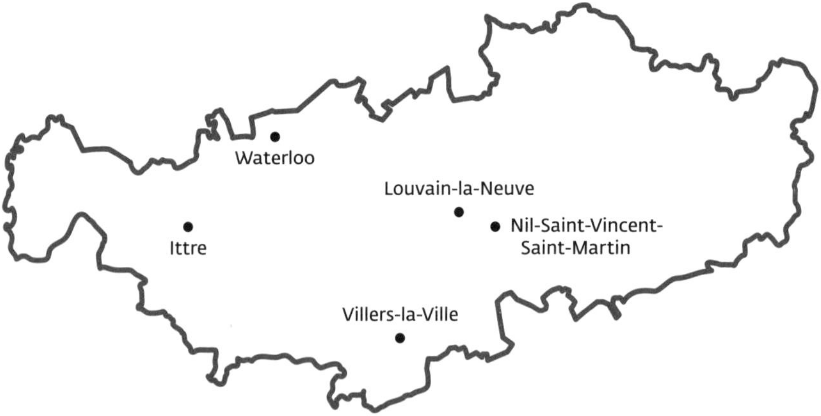

8 HAINAUT

Ploegsteert
Ellezelles
Lessines
Tournai
Brugelette
Seneffe
Houdeng-
Goegnies
Mons
Boussu
Morlanwelz
Charleroi
Mont-sur-Marchienne
Erquelinnes
Thuin

9 NAMUR

Marche-
les-Dames
Namur
Malonne
Crupet
Annevoie-Rouillon
Baillonville
Dinant
Waulsort
Hastière
Houyet
Lavaux-
Sainte-Anne
Nismes
Oignies-en-
Thiérache
Brûly-de-
Pesche
Vresse-
sur-Semois

10 LIÈGE

Petit Lanaye
Eben-Emael
Kelmis
Liège
Sart
Nessonvaux
Neupré
Francorchamps
Robertville
Leykaul
Ovifat
Malmedy
Waimes
Sankt Vith

11 LUXEMBOURG

C-MINE

ART *and* CULTURE Ⓐ

Inspiring ART MUSEUMS

1 **VERBEKE FOUNDATION**
Westakker 2
Kemzeke
East Flanders
+32 (0)3 789 22 07
verbeke foundation.com

Here is one of the strangest spots in Belgium. It looks like a junk yard next to a motorway, out in the middle of nowhere. But this unexpected location is home to one of the most astonishing private art collections in Europe.
It's not easy to find, even with the best map. You have to look out for the McDonald's sign poking above the trees. Then you might spot a small sign pointing to the Verbeke Foundation. Turn off the road here and look for a parking space among the rusting cranes and heaps of wood.
Geert Verbeke used to run a road haulage business on this site. He turned the place over to art in the summer of 2007. It has slowly evolved into a rambling, overgrown collection with strange rusting sculptures hidden among the trees and odd art creations stored in an enormous glass greenhouse.
Verbeke has acquired some striking art works over the years, including a giant vase by Andrea Branzi that once stood in the courtyard of the Ghent Design Museum, a group of realistic horse sculptures by Ronald de Winter and a collection of Theo Jansen's curious moving creatures called *Strandbeesten*.
Visitors receive a little map to navigate around the site, which lists more than 60 works dotted around the wilderness. Some are so well hidden almost no one ever finds then, like Ryan Mendoza's *The White*

House, an abandoned Detroit building in a remote clearing in the woods.

The collection also includes the vast *Archive for the Future* by the Dutch artist Jacobus Kloppenburg, which occupies a warren of little rooms inside 13 stacked shipping containers. Most of Kloppenburg's works were destroyed by Amsterdam city council when it removed 52.000 kilos of art from his house in 13 containers. Here you can see all that remains.

The Verbeke foundation provides space where artists can work on temporary projects while living in a small farmhouse. It also has a restaurant with a terrace, an artificial lake and two art installations where you can spend the night.

1 VERBEKE FOUNDATION

2 **LA BOVERIE**

Parc de la Boverie
Rue du Parc
Liège
+32 (0)4 238 55 01
laboverie.com

It used to be a forgotten art museum at the end of an island in the Meuse, but Liège's La Boverie has been reborn. The impressive domed building put up for the Liège World Fair of 1905 reopened in 2016 after a long restoration.

Liège is working to improve its image and its art museum has become a landmark building with big windows looking out on the river and a new footbridge linking it to Liège-Guillemins station. Built up over the centuries, the collection includes a beautiful painting of Le Havre harbour by Monet, along with works by Wiertz, Ensor and Magritte. But perhaps the most interesting room contains nine modern paintings declared 'degenerate art' by Hitler and sold in 1938 at an auction in Lucerne. A delegation sent from Liège snapped up the nine works, which included Picasso's sad portrait of the Soler Family sitting down to a picnic.

The museum cafe, cleverly renamed Madame Boverie, occupies a striking domed hall furnished with old industrial benches, assorted wooden chairs and plants in black metal pots. It is the perfect spot to experience the cultural renaissance of this old European city.

3 **ROGER RAVEEL MUSEUM**

Gildestraat 2-8
Machelen-aan-de-Leie
East Flanders
+32 (0)9 381 60 00
rogerraveelmuseum.be

You might sometimes be the only person wandering around the Roger Raveel Museum. But it's worth making a trip to the sleepy village of Machelen where this neglected artist spent his life. The museum is a stunning modern building by the architect Stéphane Beel joined to a former parsonage where temporary exhibitions are held in a warren of little rooms.

Raveel was an unconventional artist who created paintings using chicken wire, mirrors, window frames and bicycle wheels. He even occasionally incorporated caged yellow songbirds into his works. A short walk from the museum brings you to the cemetery where his grave is marked by a simple flat stone. His wife, who died a few years before him, has a more striking tomb overlooked by an enigmatic male sculpture with a mirror embedded in his stomach. The cemetery stands near a cut off bend in the old River Leie that would have been filled in if Raveel had not organised a protest.

4 MUSEUM MAYER VAN DEN BERGH

Lange Gasthuis-straat 19
Antwerp
+32 (0)3 338 81 88
mayer vandenbergh.be

A forgotten art collection occupies a sombre neo-Renaissance house in Antwerp. Overcome your caution and you will discover one of the finest private art collections in Europe. It was assembled by Fritz Mayer van den Bergh, a rich art collector who died at an early age, leaving everything to his mother. She turned her son's empty house, which he never occupied, into a museum. The collection includes Pieter Bruegel's haunting painting *Dulle Griet* as well as a tiny sculptured head of Blanche de France, daughter of the king of France, who died before her third birthday, just 17 days after her sister passed away. Their devastated father commissioned a marble tomb with the figures of his two daughters. It was destroyed in the French Revolution, leaving just this one little head in a deserted museum in Antwerp.

5 MARIEMONT MUSEUM

Chaussée de Mariemont 100
Morlanwelz
Hainaut
+32 (0)64 21 21 93
musee-mariemont.be

The striking Mariemont Museum is the last thing you would expect to find in the old industrial region around Charleroi. Located in a landscaped park where a 16th-century castle once stood, it contains an extraordinary collection created by the fabulously rich industrialist Raoul Warocqué. He accumulated thousands of objects on his travels, including a decorated room from Pompeii, a giant Egyptian God and dozens of classical Greek statues. The collection was gifted to the Belgian state when Warocqué died in 1917. But disaster struck after the old château was destroyed by fire in 1960, leaving just one wing standing. The collection survived and is now displayed in a severe concrete building designed by the Belgian architect Roger Bastin. The museum sits in a romantic park with the overgrown ruins of an 18th-century château, a hidden temple, rose garden and a version of Rodin's famous *Burghers of Calais*.

6 MUSÉE DE LA PHOTOGRAPHIE

Avenue Paul Pastur 11
Mont-sur-Marchienne
Hainaut
+32 (0)71 43 58 10
museephoto.be

This beautiful photography museum occupies a restored convent in the Charleroi suburbs. It is a wonderful building to wander around, with an outstanding collection of 80.000 photographs, along with a bright cafe and a shady terraced garden where you can eat a simple lunch.

6 MUSÉE DE LA PHOTOGRAPHIE

7 LE GRAND-HORNU

Rue Ste-Louise 82
Boussu
Hainaut
+32 (0)65 65 21 21
grand-hornu.eu

The vast Grand-Hornu industrial site was founded in the early 19th century as an utopian mining village in the heart of the Borinage district. The rugged brick architecture has been lovingly restored to house the contemporary art museum MAC's and the design museum CID. It is a little tricky to find, but worth making a trip out here to wander through the impressive neoclassical buildings, visit surprising art exhibitions and follow a wild nature trail to the top of the abandoned slag heap.

7 LE GRAND-HORNU

ARTISTS' HOUSES

8 **WIERTZ MUSEUM**
Rue Vautier 62
Ixelles
Brussels
+32 (0)2 648 17 18
fine-arts-museum.be

A French travel magazine once listed the Wiertz Museum in Brussels as one of the most beautiful in the world. And so it is. The only problem is almost no one knows about it. The museum is located in a forgotten corner of the city, hidden away behind the European Parliament. And it is filled with paintings no one likes.

The museum was originally built in 1851 as a studio for the Belgian romantic painter Antoine Wiertz. He chose to settle in an unfashionable location on the edge of the city, and came up with a cunning arrangement to pay for the house and studio. In 1850, he wrote to the Belgian interior minister offering to donate all his unsold paintings to the state if they funded the building. And so the former studio became a museum after his death, displaying more than 200 of his works – all fixed permanently to the wall, as he had instructed – along with his easel and other sentimental relics.

The building is a rare example of a perfectly preserved mid-19th-century museum, with rooms lit by natural daylight and paintings protected by low brass rails. But the collection includes terrifying paintings such as *Premature Burial*, in which a man struggles to escape the coffin in which he is about to be buried.

9 JAMES ENSOR HOUSE

Vlaanderen-straat 29
Ostend
West Flanders
+32 (0)59 41 89 00
ensorstad.be

An intimate museum devoted to the provocative Ostend artist James Ensor occupies the terraced house where his aunt and uncle once ran a souvenir shop. Ensor lived in the cramped apartment above the shop from 1917 until his death in 1949. The ground floor is filled with an odd collection of shells, masks and other seaside souvenirs, while two upstairs rooms contain Ensor's battered harmonica, masks and puppets. A major renovation in 2020 by Belgian architects noArchitecten added an impressive Ensor Experience Centre next door. This contains a reconstructed studio, reproductions of Ensor's paintings and an account of the artist's strange life.

10 PANAMARENKO HOUSE

Biekorfstraat 2
Antwerp
BOOK AN APPOINTMENT TO VISIT THE HOUSE AT:
muhka.be

It's quite a challenge to get inside the former home of the Antwerp artist Panamarenko, who died in 2019. Now owned by the contemporary art museum M HKA, it is only open on Saturdays from 2 pm to 3.30 pm, for small groups of visitors. But it is worth trying to book a visit to see inside this eccentric artist's town house and garage, where he lived for more than 30 years along with his mother, six parrots and a collection of aircraft parts. Panamarenko (who took his name from Pan Am airlines) spent his life building strange flying machines, replica submarines and mechanical chickens. His home is filled with odd dusty objects, old toys and haunting poetic works. The elicopter platform on the roof is a final touch of madness.

11 MAGRITTE HOUSE

RENÉ MAGRITTE MUSEUM

Rue Esseghem 135
Jette
Brussels
+32 (0)2 428 26 26
magrittemuseum.be

The surrealist artist René Magritte lived for 24 years in a modest apartment in Brussels, along with his wife Georgette and a fluffy Pomeranian dog. The artist's former home, where he painted more than half his works, is now a fascinating little museum.

It lies in a quiet Brussels street where you would imagine nothing ever happens. But then you notice a small black nameplate marked Magritte and a solitary street lamp outside the house copied from Magritte's painting *The Empire of Light*.

Magritte and Georgette moved here in 1930, soon after they returned from an unsuccessful period in Paris. The house is furnished with department store antiques, comfortable sofas and a baby grand piano. Magritte worked in the tiny kitchen at the back of the house, painting at an easel he had to move aside when Georgette served dinner.

Several details in the house are familiar from famous Magrittes. His painting *The Forbidden Reading* includes the very staircase you see in front of you in the hallway. Another work called *Time Transfixed*, in which a steam locomotive emerges from a fireplace, includes a fireplace like the one in the couple's front room.

The first floor of the museum is filled with documents, photographs and odd mementoes, including the plastic doorbell from the Magritte's final home in Schaerbeek.

12 PAUL DELVAUX MUSEUM

P. Delvauxlaan 42
Koksijde
West Flanders
+32 (0)58 52 12 29
delvauxmuseum.com

Located in the little beach town of Sint-Idesbald, the Paul Delvaux Museum stands next to the tiny whitewashed fisherman's cottage where Delvaux spent the final years of his life. Recently renovated, the museum owns the world's largest collection of paintings by this mysterious artist. The works reveal his obsessive interest in classical architecture, nude women and deserted train stations.

The museum is a quiet, enigmatic place furnished with wooden benches from old Belgian trains. Its rooms are bathed in a mysterious light that adds to the melancholy mood.

Creative

CULTURAL VENUES

13 BPS22

Bd Solvay 22
Charleroi
Hainaut
+32 (0)71 27 29 71
bps22.be

The BPS22 museum offers a sneak preview of Charleroi's ambitious plans for the future. It occupies a massive neoclassical building on a rather desolate square in the upper town. The overbearing School of Labour on the other side has seen better days, but BPS22 has injected creative energy to this area of Charleroi since it opened a few years ago. Located in a building created for the 1911 Charleroi expo, the museum displays Hainaut province's contemporary art collection in a vast glass-roofed exhibition hall.

14 HET PREDIKHEREN

Goswin de Stassartstraat 88
Mechelen
Antwerp
+32 (0)15 40 44 70
hetpredikheren.mechelen.be

An ancient 17th-century baroque monastery in Mechelen has been radically transformed into a public library. Left to rot since the 1970s, the building was finally rescued in 2019 by the Rotterdam architect Mechthild Stuhlmacher. She has preserved intriguing traces from the past, including faded wallpaper, ancient wood beams and old gravestones. They recall the building's history as a monastery, barracks, weapons store and military hospital. The architect went on to reshape the monumental building with polished stone floors, subtle wood fittings and a fabulous children's library. The result is a warm, complex building where visitors can browse the shelves, drink a coffee and listen to a Sunday concert.

15 C-MINE

C-Mine 10
Genk
Limburg
+32 (0)89 65 44 90
c-mine.be

A huge mine complex on the edge of Genk has been turned into a magnificent centre of contemporary culture. The impressive old mine buildings from 1917 have been preserved, including an engine house full of oily machinery, the lamp room and managers' building, as well as two skeletal pit heads. The complex now incorporates a cinema, several restaurants, a tourist office and a huge metal maze.

15 C-MINE

16 Z33

Bonnenfanten-straat 1
Hasselt
Limburg
+32 (0)11 29 59 60
z33.be

Named after its former address (Zuivelmarkt 33), this exciting contemporary art space exhibits works by international designers and artists in a modernist exhibition hall dating from 1938. Temporary exhibitions make creative use of the building's vast empty spaces, but art is also displayed in the nearby Begijnhof houses, in the streets of Hasselt and out in the countryside between Hasselt and Genk.
A new expansion opened in 2020 in the Begijnhof garden. Designed by Italian architect Francesca Torzo, it is meant to evoke the mood of a mediaeval town with little squares, alleys and a fountain. The building won the Italian Architecture Prize in 2020 and caught the eye of *The Guardian* architecture critic Rowan Moore, who listed it as one of the five best buildings of 2020.

17 UTOPIA

Utopia 1
Aalst
East Flanders
+32 (0)53 72 38 51
utopia.aalst.be

Aalst's stunning city library opened in 2018 in an abandoned corner of the old industrial city. The name recalls Aalst printer Dirk Martens' role in bringing out the first edition of Thomas More's *Utopia*. Designed by Dutch firm KAAN Architecten, the building incorporates three concrete levels that appear to float above the atrium, wood bookshelves that rise through the floors and illuminated images from Martens' 1516 edition of *Utopia*. The complex embraces a former 19th-century military cadet school now occupied by an academy of performing arts, so you might spot a student playing a violin or a dance performance in a rehearsal space. Enclosed by three new urban squares, Aalst's library has revitalised an entire neighbourhood. You might even call it Utopian.

19 CONCERTGEBOUW

18 DE GROTE POST

Hendrik Serruys-laan 18-A
Ostend
West Flanders
+32 (0)59 33 90 00
degrotepost.be

Ostend's modernist post office closed down in 1999 and lay empty for many years until the city finally decided to turn it into a cultural centre. The Antwerp architects B-architecten lovingly restored the modernist details such as the post office counters and phone booths, but added some striking new elements. The building now draws audiences with an adventurous programme of theatre, dance, comedy and concerts.

19 CONCERTGEBOUW

't Zand 34
Bruges
West Flanders
+32 (0)50 47 69 99
concertgebouw.be

The new Concertgebouw (concert building) in Bruges was built in 2002 by the Ghent architects Paul Robbrecht and Hilde Daem. The striking rust-red concert hall was the first truly innovative building in Bruges since the 15th century. But it came as a brutal shock for many in this old town of Gothic church spires and tiny almshouses. The concert hall still looks out of place, although it has established an inspiring cultural programme.

Art in

UNEXPECTED PLACES

20 **THE GRIEVING PARENTS**

VLADSLO CEMETERY

Houtlandstraat 3

Diksmuide

West Flanders

The German cemetery at Vladslo is a quiet place in the Flemish countryside where few people ever go. It contains the graves of 25.638 German soldiers who died in this region of Belgium, including the 18-year-old son of the Berlin sculptor Käthe Kollwitz.
Peter Kollwitz died near Diksmuide on 23 October 1914 when the war had hardly begun. On that day, the German army was launching a series of savage attacks in an attempt to break through the British trenches around Ypres. Thousands of young German students marched into battle singing patriotic songs. But many of them were killed almost immediately, like 18-year-old Peter Kollwitz. The Germans refer to this futile battle as the Massacre of the Innocents. Peter was buried under a simple wooden cross in a nearby cemetery called Friedhof Roggeveld along with another 1558 soldiers. The cemetery was closed down in 1954 and the bodies were moved to the massive Vladslo Cemetery, where more than 25.000 German soldiers are buried. And Friedhof Roggeveld vanished from the map.
Just a few days after she learned of her son's death, Käthe Kollwitz began to work on sketches for a memorial. Many years later, she completed a powerful work featuring two enormous granite figures modelled on herself and her husband.

21 THE WALLOONS

JARDINS DU MAÏEUR

Rue de Fer

Namur

No sign. Nothing. Only locals know about the mural hidden in the garden behind the new town hall in Namur. But it's worth taking a look at this trompe-l'oeil fresco by the French collective CitéCréation. Painted in 2004 to illustrate Walloon identity, it features celebrities such as Charlemagne and Georges Simenon. Other aspects of Walloon identity are represented by book titles, paintings and street festivals.

22 MEMENTO

BORGLOON CEMETERY

Lambertusstraat

Borgloon

Limburg

borgloon.be

A strange art installation stands in the middle of Borgloon's cemetery. The artist Wesley Meuris has created a circular steel pavilion with narrow openings that provide views of the surrounding countryside. The work forms part of a project by Hasselt art centre Z33 to place modern sculpture in the landscape around Borgloon. Located close to cycle point 152.

23 PANNENHUIS METRO STATION

Rue Charles Demeer

Brussels

stib.be

The Brussels metro has stunning underground stations decorated by 60 contemporary Belgian artists. Most people barely glance at the art as they rush for a train. But there are many striking artworks that can be enjoyed for the price of a metro ticket. One of the most impressive stops is Pannenhuis station in northern Brussels where the entrance hall is decorated with a bright orange art installation like something from a science fiction movie. In recent years it has become a favourite venue for fashion shoots and Instagram posts.

Singular SCULPTURES

24 THE DIVER

PORT DES YACHTS

Boulevard Frère-Orban
Liège

Balanced on his hands on top of a giant steel arc, the muscular figure *Le Plongeur* (The Diver) was placed on the banks of the Meuse in Liège in 2000. But the work was actually made 60 years earlier by the young Romanian sculptor Idel Ianchelevici, who copied a figure he had made for the 1939 International Water Expo. When war broke out, the project was abandoned and the copy lay forgotten in the basement of the fine art museum until 1998. This spectacular modern sculpture now stands close to the original site on the banks of the Meuse.

25 LUCKY LUKE

PARC REINE ASTRID

Boulevard Audent
Charleroi
Hainaut

The derelict industrial town of Charleroi is working on its image by installing bright statues of Belgian comic book figures in locations around the old centre. You can spot the cowboy Lucky Luke on the edge of the city park, the weird invented animal Marsupilami on top of a fountain and the comic characters Boule and Bill in the middle of a roundabout. Several metro stations are also decorated with scenes from comic books published in Charleroi.

26 MOTHER EARTH I

Dorp
Sint-Martens-Latem
East Flanders

It is not easy to find *Mother Earth I*. The massive bronze nude lies half buried behind the town hall in the former artists' village of Sint-Martens-Latem. It was put here in 2007 by the Kortrijk artist Ann Deman in a quiet meadow planted with apple trees, next to a landing stage on the River Leie. A few years later, she placed a second version titled *Mother Earth II* in a park beside the Leie in Kortrijk.

27 ARC MAJEUR

E411 motorway
Lavaux-Sainte-Anne
Namur

An enormous steel structure resembling a broken ring rises above the E411 motorway in a remote region of the Ardennes. Designed in 1984 by French artist Bernar Venet, *Arc Majeur* was originally conceived for a French site, but local politicians rejected the idea. More than three decades later, the John Cockerill Foundation funded the construction of the 250-ton sculpture. Located on the main motorway between Brussels and Luxembourg, it is the world's tallest public artwork – twice the height of Rio de Janeiro's *Christ the Redeemer*.

Forbidden **ART**

28 **TEMPLE OF THE HUMAN PASSIONS**
CINQUANTENAIRE PARK
Brussels
kmkg-mrah.be

In 1899 the Brussels sculptor Jef Lambeaux carved an enormous frieze called *Les Passions Humaines* out of 17 blocks of pure white Carrara marble. It featured dozens of naked bodies symbolising human passions and sins such as joy, seduction, suicide and rape. Once the work was finished, it was placed inside a neat neoclassical temple built in the Cinquantenaire Park by the young architect Victor Horta.

But the work was controversial even before it was carved. When Lambeaux produced an early sketch, the art magazine *l'Art Moderne* condemned it as "a pile of naked and contorted bodies, chaotic and vague, bloated and pretentious, pompous and empty". The Belgian public was equally shocked when the work was finally unveiled. Three days later, the temple was closed to the public and the entrance boarded up.

More than a century later, the frieze is still hidden behind a solid wall. But the building is now open on certain days in the summer. Otherwise, you can peer through the keyhole to see what caused all the fuss. Information on opening times at the Art & History Museum.

29 ADAM AND EVE PANELS

GHENT CATHEDRAL
Sint-Baafsplein
Ghent
East Flanders
sintbaafs kathedraal.be

When Jan van Eyck unveiled his enormous altarpiece *The Adoration of the Mystic Lamb* (*Het Lam Gods*) in 1432, it included two side panels with the naked figures of Adam and Eve. For several centuries, the figures offended no one, until Emperor Joseph II of Austria saw them during a visit to Ghent in 1781. He ordered them to be taken down, and replaced by copies with the figures dressed in ridiculous bearskins. The originals were put back in 1946, and the copies now hang in Ghent Cathedral in a spot where almost no one ever spots them.

29 ADAM AND EVE PANELS

30 FÉLICIEN ROPS MUSEUM

Rue Fumal 12
Namur
+32 (0)81 77 67 55
museerops.be

One of the most scandalous artists of the 19th century, Félicien Rops was born in Namur in 1833. A gifted artist, he shocked people with his erotic paintings of lecherous priests, Parisian prostitutes and women being molested by snakes. After his marriage broke up, he lived with two sisters in Paris. Some of his most decadent works now hang in an elegant 18th-century town house once owned by Rops' parents-in-law. Established in 1964, the museum displays his paintings and engravings in a series of dark rooms. You discover everything from early caricatures to his late decadent works, along with more risqué works hidden away in drawers. The museum occasionally organises exhibitions on Rops linking him to Symbolists such as James Ensor and Edvard Munch.

31 LEOPOLD II STATUES

Koning Albert I Park
Halle
Flemish Brabant

TOWN HALL
Grote Markt
Leuven
Flemish Brabant

There are countless monuments celebrating the former Belgian king Leopold II who reigned from 1865 to 1909. But many were attacked in the summer of 2020 as part of Black Lives Matter protests across the world. The activists condemned the king for his policies in the Congo where he ruthlessly exploited the country as his own private colony. In Halle, a bust of Leopold was stolen from a local park, but later returned to its pedestal with a notice attached informing people of his crimes. In November 2020, Leuven city council removed a statue of Leopold II from the Gothic town hall. The 19th-century statue ended up in the building's basement, leaving an empty niche on the town hall façade.

Wild STREET ART

32 SINT-DIMPNA HOSPITAL

J.B. Stessens-straat 2
Geel
Antwerp

The Belgian street artist Bart Smeets, who signs his works Smates, produced an astonishing mural in 2019 on a wall of the Sint-Dimpna hospital in Geel. The 20-metre-high photorealist portrait shows a child looking over a wall at the moon.

33 BRUGBERGPAD

Brugbergpad
Kessel-Lo
Flemish Brabant

A team of 20 young street artists repainted a 175-metre-long concrete wall in Kessel-Lo in the summer of 2021. Many of the artists have brought a feminist vibe to the wall including Stina De Roeck, Warsnoes and Art of MAU.

34 BERCHEM STATION

Burgemeester Ryckaertsplein 1
Berchem
Antwerp
streetartantwerp.com

Striking street art can be seen on walls of Berchem station in Antwerp. The Belgian street artist who signs his works Cazn has created large works inspired by Antwerp icons on the walls of platforms 6 and 7. Other artists have added works along the tracks leading to Antwerp Central Station.

35 SLEEPING ANIMALS

Hofstraat and other locations
Ostend
West Flanders
thecrystalship.org

Ostend is dotted with street art that appeared in 2016 during The Crystal Ship festival. You can find enormous works on the side walls of apartment buildings, but also tiny works hidden in unexpected spots. The Ghent artist ROA came to town to paint a heap of sleeping animals next to an abandoned site used as car park. On an adjacent wall, the Spanish artist Isaac Cordal attached a tiny figure of a man on a balcony.

Ostend tourist office has produced a map that pinpoints 68 works around the city, including recent additions by Sozyone, Kitsune and Toykyo. The map is essential. Without it, you might not find anything at all.

35 SLEEPING ANIMALS

FORT NAPOLEON

HISTORY

36 BRÛLY-DE-PESCHE

Brûly-de-Pesche
Namur

Brûly-de-Pesche is a tiny village in the Ardennes reached along a deserted road. You could easily pass through without realising anything about its extraordinary history. But stop to look at the information board near the church and you begin to realise the importance of this place.

It began in the early summer of 1940 when German troops evacuated 28 villages in the region, including Brûly-de-Pesche, forcing 27.000 people out of their homes. It was the start of one of the largest secret operations of the Second World War. For 22 days, this tiny village near the French border became Hitler's command centre for the invasion of France.

The village is still dotted with buildings briefly occupied by the Nazi leaders. The local school became a command centre where generals bent over large maps as tanks moved closer to Paris. The church was converted into a cinema where Hitler would watch German propaganda newsreels on a screen put up in front of the altar.

A massive concrete bunker was built in the woods to protect Hitler from air attacks. Two Bavarian chalets were constructed nearby as a canteen and officers' mess. The trees around the bunker were painted with white fluorescent stripes to mark a route through the woods in the dark. They led to a stone amphitheatre and a small pool in a clearing

where Hitler met military leaders such as Göring and Von Ribbentrop.
Most of these places where history was made are still standing, including the path near the church where Hitler performed a little dance after he was told France had fallen and the church where the surrender document was translated into French and typed out.
The site was forgotten for many years until a new visitors centre opened in 2015. Its focus is less on Hitler's brutal invasion plan and more on the lives of ordinary Belgian families forced to leave their homes in 1940. It includes a fascinating section on resistance fighters who hid in the forest at the end of the war. Once you have visited the site, you can follow hiking trails in the woods or eat lunch in the friendly local restaurant La Fontaine.

37 THE FATAL ROCK

Marche-les-Dames
Namur

A quiet path runs through the woods to the rocks where King Albert I fell to his death in 1934. You get there across a railway line and then up a steep trail through the trees. The *rocher fatal* (death rock) is closed off by a low wall to stop people getting too close. There is nothing to say what happened in this haunting, forgotten spot.
The country woke up to hear the news on the radio on the morning of 18 February. The king had fallen while climbing alone near the village of Marche-les-Dames. It made no sense. He was an experienced climber who had tackled some of the hardest peaks in the Alps, so why did he fall during a simple beginner's ascent? Some people still believe in a conspiracy.

A small museum was created at the foot of the rocks, but it closed down some years ago. The only memorial is a cross on the slope marking the spot where the body was found and a hedge clipped to form the letter A.

38 FORT LIEFKENSHOEK

Ketenislaan 4
Kallo
Antwerp
+32 (0)3 750 12 90
fortliefkenshoek.be

Built by the Dutch in 1579, the old fort at Liefkenshoek is now surrounded by monstrous oil and chemical installations. But once you have crossed the moat, you find yourself inside a perfectly-preserved star-shaped fortification. A large semi-circular barracks from the Napoleonic period has been turned into a museum with rooms devoted to different periods in Liefkenshoek's history. The building was for a time used as a quarantine hospital for emigrants bound for the United States, then a barracks and finally a vacation centre for military families. The grounds have recently been planted with trees to create a little nature reserve in the menacing industrial landscape. And you can eat well in a dark Flemish tavern located in the former gatehouse. Free entry.

39 CABLE CAR CABIN

L'Extérieur Nuit
Place du Chanoine Descamps 6
Namur
+32 (0)81 23 09 09
fenetresurcour.be

Look out in Namur for an old metal sign that reads *Téléférique 50m*. It leads into the courtyard of a former industrial building in the heart of the old town. Here you find a 1956 Swiss cable car cabin suspended above a restaurant terrace. The last of the iconic red cabins known locally as 'eggs', it used to carry tourists up to the Namur citadel. The cable car closed in 1997 due to falling rocks and was destroyed by fire in 2002, leaving just this solitary relic.

39 **CABLE CAR CABIN**

40 MORESNET VIADUCT

La Calamine
Liège

The impressive iron viaduct near the town of La Calamine/Kelmis was constructed during the First World War to carry German troops rapidly to the Western front. The work was mainly done by captured Russian soldiers working in terrible conditions. The local museum in La Calamine contains odd ornaments made by the prisoners out of old shell cases, and the local cemetery has graves of nine Russians who died of unknown causes. The bridge was destroyed by the Belgian army in 1940 to slow down the German invasion. It was later rebuilt by the German army, but destroyed again in 1944. The third version, built after the war, is still used to carry goods trains high above the town.

41 FORT NAPOLEON

Vuurtorenweg 13
Ostend
West Flanders
+32 (0)59 33 09 37
fort-napoleon.be

Take the free ferry across Ostend harbour and follow the signs to Fort Napoleon. You come to a massive brick fortress built in the dunes by Napoleon and occupied by German soldiers in the Second World War. The building was superbly restored in 2006 by the Bruges architects Govaert & Vanhoutte to create a fortress museum and brasserie with a terrace looking out on the dunes.

Haunting

WAR CEMETERIES

42 SAINT SYMPHORIEN MILITARY CEMETERY

Rue N. Dehon 32
Mons
Hainaut

A war cemetery in the fields outside Mons contains the graves of 284 German and 229 British and Commonwealth soldiers buried together in a romantic wooded setting. The cemetery was begun by the German army in late 1914 to bury soldiers from both sides who died near Mons. It contains the grave of the first British soldier killed in the war, but also, remarkably, the last British soldier to die. He was shot just two minutes before the war officially ended at 11 am on 11 November 1918. On 4 August 2014, leaders from Germany, Belgium, France and the United Kingdom gathered here in a moving ceremony to mark the one hundredth anniversary of the outbreak of war.

43 ARDENNES AMERICAN CEMETERY

Route du Condroz 164
Neupré
Liège

The American Cemetery at Neupré on the edge of the Ardennes is normally deserted. But occasionally a visitor comes to wander among the neat rows of simple white stone crosses. They mark the graves of 5328 American soldiers who died in Belgium in the Second World War, mostly during the bitter 1944 winter offensive fought in the forests around Bastogne. A memorial chapel occupies a square white building decorated with a huge American eagle. Inside are three large wall maps showing the course of the war in Europe.

44 HEDGE ROW TRENCH CEMETERY

Verbrandemolen-straat
Zillebeke
West Flanders

This is possibly the most beautiful of all the First World War cemeteries in Belgium. Hidden in the Palingbeek woods, it is a silent, haunting place reached along a forest track. The original cemetery was destroyed by shellfire and the graves were laid out after the war in a circle. Three army packs are lined up outside the wall, with objects once carried by the soldiers, including gas masks, handkerchiefs and even makeup.

45 LANGEMARK GERMAN WAR CEMETERY

Klerkenstraat 64
Langemark
West Flanders

The vast German cemetery at Langemark is entered by a sober black pavilion designed by Belgian architects Govaert & Vanhoutte. Here you can watch historical films on three screens before entering the cemetery along a path lined with willows. This is a quiet and melancholy place dotted with rugged stone crosses. The soldiers' names are carved in small letters on stones that lie flat on the ground. There are no personal details, nothing to say who they were, or where they died. Many of the dead were young volunteer students who joined the German army in the early years of the war. More than 44.000 soldiers are buried here, yet you can sometimes be the only visitor.

46 ENCLOS DES FUSILLÉS

Rue Colonel Bourg 102
Schaerbeek
Brussels

No one knows about this cemetery hidden in a wood behind the Flemish broadcasting building in Brussels. A quiet cobbled lane leads to the spot known as the 'Enclos des Fusillés'. This forgotten spot is the site of a firing range where Belgian resistance fighters were executed during two world wars. A total of 342 small concrete crosses commemorate the victims, including the Belgian spy Gabrielle Petit, who was shot here in 1916, and the British nurse Edith Cavell, who died here in 1915.

47 RECOGNE GERMAN WAR CEMETERY

Recogne
Luxembourg

A quiet road near the Ardennes village of Foy leads to a haunting German war cemetery with hundreds of dark stone crosses laid out among the trees. Created in 1947, the site marks the graves of 6807 soldiers killed in the attack on Bastogne in 1944-45. The crosses are each inscribed with six names, the youngest victim being 17 years old.

48 PALINGBEEK

Palingbeekstraat 18
Zillebeke
West Flanders
+32 (0)57 23 08 40

The Palingbeek nature reserve stands on a ridge south of Ypres heavily shelled in the First World War. The landscape has been sensitively restored to create a beautiful nature reserve. You can follow trails to reach military sites and forgotten cemeteries deep in the woods, occasionally glimpsing the reconstructed spires of Ypres in the distance. Begin at the café De Palingbeek.

49 EBEN-EMAEL FORTRESS

Rue du Fort 40
Eben-Emael
Liège
+32 (0)4 286 28 61
fort-eben-emael.be

An enormous Belgian military complex is hidden below the Sint-Pietersberg near the village of Eben-Emael. Built in 1935 close to the Dutch border, this massive concrete fortification was designed to protect a weak point on the Belgian frontier. One of the largest military structures ever built, it comprised 17 bunkers linked by a network of underground tunnels.

On the eve of World War Two, Eben-Emael was like an underground town, with kitchens, bedrooms, showers, a hospital and even a barber shop. It was considered the strongest fort in Europe, yet on 10 May 1940 a small team of German paratroopers landed on the roof in gliders and captured the stronghold in less than 15 minutes. The abandoned and crumbling fort is still owned by the army, but certain parts have been converted into a military museum.

50 BAYERNWALD

Voormezelestraat 2
Wijtschate,
Heuvelland
West Flanders
TICKETS AT:
Sint-Laurentius-plein 1
Kemmel
+32 (0)57 45 04 55
toerismeheuvelland.be

The Bayernwald trenches were constructed in 1916 by German troops along the high ground to the south of Ypres. Forgotten after the war, the bunkers were uncovered in 1971 by a local school teacher. The site was restored as a museum in 2004, although it is not the easiest place to visit. Tickets have to be bought in advance at the Kemmel tourist office.

51 SINT ELOI CRATER

Rijselseweg
(near Eekhofstraat)
Voormezele
West Flanders
+32 (0)57 23 92 20
toerismeieper.be

You can track down the remains of 16 craters created along the Messines Ridge by huge underground mines detonated at 3.10 am on 7 June 1917. The Sint Eloi Crater was produced by the largest of the underground mines. It is now a quiet spot with an abandoned British bunker. Almost no one comes here, but you can enter the site by asking at the Ypres tourist office for an access code.

Enigmatic MONUMENTS

52 **BIRCH TREE CIRCLE**

FORÊT DE SOIGNES
Drève de l'Infante
Uccle
Brussels

It's not easy to find this monument. Deep in the forest outside Brussels, 32 young birch trees were planted in a circle in memory of the victims of two terrorist attacks in Brussels on 22 March 2016. The memorial was created by the landscape architect Bas Smets in the middle of a clearing. The trees are equally spaced to create the impression of people standing in a circle holding hands. They surround a stone circle made of 32 blocks of polished blue limestone.
You can reach the site by a footbridge over a lake called Étang des Enfants Noyés, literally, the Lake of Drowned Children. The route across this quiet pond was inspired by the ancient Greek legend of the dead who are ferried across the River Styx.
Take tram 8 to Coccinelles.

53 **PEACE WOOD**

Foy
Luxembourg

The area around Bastogne is dotted with relics of the Battle of the Bulge, including cemeteries, memorials and abandoned tanks. But the Peace Wood planted in 2005 to mark the sixtieth anniversary of the battle is less well known. It is reached down a deserted road near the village of Foy. The trees were planted in the shape of UNICEF's symbol of a mother and child. Several hundred trees have small stones next to them with names of former soldiers who have visited

the site. But perhaps the most touching memorial is a small group of 28 trees planted in memory of children and teachers killed in the 2012 Sandy Hook massacre.
Located on a small road off the Foy to Bizory route.

54 CENTRE OF BELGIUM

Rue de la Planchette
Ittre
Walloon Brabant

Tiège
Nil-Saint-Vincent-Saint-Martin
Walloon Brabant

Most Belgians have been taught that the village of Ittre, south of Brussels, is the geographical centre of their country. A large millstone in the centre of the village marks the precise spot. But it is wrong. The true centre moved about 30 kilometres when the East Cantons were handed to Belgium in 1919. No one noticed the mistake until 1998, when a small pyramid was placed in a field near the village of Nil-Saint-Vincent-Saint-Martin to mark the true spot. But the old monument has been left in Ittre.

55 CHRISTMAS TRUCE CROSS

Chemin du Mont de la Hutte
Ploegsteert
Hainaut

A small wooden cross stands next to a quiet country road near Ploegsteert Wood. It was put up a few years ago to commemorate the Christmas Truce in 1914 when soldiers on both sides stopped fighting and began to sing Christmas carols. Some climbed out of the trenches to bury the dead, shook hands with the enemy and exchanged little gifts. They also played a game of football in a cabbage field, which was apparently won by the German side. In recent years, this remote spot has become a shrine where people leave footballs, team stripes and souvenir mugs.

56 FORMER CENTRE OF THE EU

Rue R. Delizée 102
Oignies-en-Thiérache
Namur

A forgotten monument known as the Cathedral of Light stands in a forest clearing near the village of Oignies. Located in a remote area of southern Belgium near the French border, it marks the official geographical centre of the European Union between 1995 and 2004. A path leads through the trees to a glass monument, which is surrounded by 15 low columns marked with the names of the EU member states at the time. The columns are placed at different distances from the centre depending on when they joined the EU.

The only building in this remote forested area of Belgium is an abandoned roadside restaurant named Le Trou du Diable. Back in 1995, the owner tried to attract tourists, but business dropped off sharply after ten new countries joined the EU in 2004, and the geographical centre moved further east. The restaurant finally closed down in 2017.

The Trou du Diable takes its name from a local rock formation known as the Devil's Hole. A battle was fought near this site in 1914 between French and German troops. The victims are buried in a remote cemetery near here.

57 MONUMENT TO THE FORESTRY WORKERS

FORÊT DE SOIGNES
Grasdellepad
Uccle
Brussels

A quiet trail in the forest south of Brussels leads to a massive stone dolmen surrounded by a circle of 11 standing stones. It looks as if it might date from the same period as Stonehenge, but it was actually put up in 1920 in memory of Belgian forestry workers who died fighting in the First World War.

The massive stones for this unusual war memorial were brought from a neolithic quarry in the hills above Wéris village in the Ardennes.

Take the train to Groenendaal station.

Remarkable **RUINS**

58 IMPERIA CAR FACTORY

Rue Gomélevay 52
Nessonvaux
Liège

Built in 1907, the abandoned Imperia car factory dominates the village of Nessonvaux. It was established in the valley of the Vesdre by an engineer who invented one of the first hybrid car engines as well as the electric cigarette lighter. The factory originally tested its cars on local roads, but people started to complain. The owner then came up with the original idea of building a test track on the factory roof, a few years before Fiat built its famous rooftop track in Turin. The factory finally closed in 1958, leaving an impressive main building in the style of a mediaeval castle. Now there are just 34 Imperia cars left in the world, including four cars in a small museum a few kilometres down the road in the village of Fraipont. The fries shop La Friterie Imperia at Rue Docteur Heuze 339 has nostalgic photographs on its walls and the Rue Heid Mawet leads to a viewpoint where you can look down on the race track.

59 VILLERS-LA-VILLE

Rue de l'Abbaye 55
Villers-la-Ville
Walloon Brabant
+32 (0)71 88 09 80
villers.be

Hidden in a remote wooded valley, Villers-la-Ville was one of the great abbeys of Europe, but it is now a vast, silent ruin. Founded by Cistercian monks in the Middle Ages, this massive abbey was abandoned after the French Revolution. The buildings are now in ruins, overgrown with ivy, populated by wild birds. But the romantic setting comes to life on two summer nights every year when a choir performs in the floodlit ruins.

60 ROYAL D'ARDENNE STATION

Houyet
Namur

Hardly anyone knows the story of the abandoned railway station near the village of Houyet. No train has stopped here since the station closed down more than a century ago. It was built in the style of a mediaeval castle by Leopold II, who was known as the Builder King because he commissioned a great number of buildings and public works. Unfortunately, the necessary funding for these projects mostly came from his brutal exploitation of the Congo Free State.

The isolated halt was intended for guests of the luxurious 200-room hotel Chateau Royal d'Ardenne. The project was supposed to bring wealthy tourists to the Ardennes. But the station closed in 1919 and the hotel was destroyed by fire in 1968, leaving just the mysterious Gothic station hidden in the woods.

From Houyet, follow the path on the right bank of the river, direction Gendron-Gare.

61 NAMUR CITADEL STADIUM

NAMUR CITADEL
Route Merveilleuse 64
Namur
+32 (0)81 24 73 70
citadelle.namur.be

Ludus Pro Patria – Games for the Fatherland, it says on an abandoned building on the hill above Namur. This enigmatic structure turns out to be a former sport stadium opened in the early 20th century by King Leopold II. His plan was to turn the old citadel site, which no longer served any military purpose, into a centre for culture and sport.

Modelled on an ancient Greek stadium, it was designed by the Brussels architect Georges Hobé in the style of the Vienna Secession. One of the earliest reinforced concrete buildings in the country, it could seat 4000 spectators.

At the back of the stadium, hidden in the trees, there is also a concrete open-air theatre that could seat 2800 people. Now it is totally forgotten.

61 **NAMUR CITADEL STADIUM**

62 SAINT BAVO'S ABBEY

Voorhoutkaai
Ghent
East Flanders
sintbaafsabdij.stad.gent

The ruined Saint Bavo's Abbey (Sint-Baafsabdij) is a strange, forgotten building near the River Leie. Founded in the 7th century, it takes its name from a local monk who lived as a hermit in a hollow tree near Ghent. It grew into one of the most important abbeys in northern Europe, but was largely destroyed in 1540 when Charles V built a fortress on the site for his Spanish troops. A few of the abbey buildings were spared, including the cloisters, a chapel and an impressive dining hall. The baffling, overgrown ruins became a lapidary museum in 1887 filled with unidentified fragments of old buildings.

UNDERGROUND *places*

63 KEIZERSBASTION

Frankrijklei
Antwerp

The remains of a 16th-century renaissance bastion are hidden deep below the streets in an Antwerp car park. The stone structure, built during the Spanish occupation, was uncovered near the National Bank in 2003. The city decided to sacrifice a few parking spaces to create a small underground museum incorporating a stretch of the historic wall. Opened in 2017, it includes details from old maps, along with objects uncovered from the moat such as nails, coins and shoes. Entrance at Maria Henriettalei. Parking level minus 3. Open permanently.

63 KEIZERSBASTION

64 ANTWERP SEWERS

RUIHUIS
Suikerrui 21
Antwerp
+32 (0)3 344 07 55
ruien.be

Rows of green rubber boots are lined up at the entrance to the Antwerp sewers. You need to put on a pair when you take a guided walking tour through the hidden network of underground waterways known as *Ruien*. The two-hour visit offers a fascinating insight into these mediaeval canals that once ran through the city. There are signs along the way to indicate the streets above your head. Tours are sometimes cancelled after heavy rain, as the sewers can become flooded.

65 BUNKER IN THE BRUSSELS PARK

PARC DE BRUXELLES/ WARANDEPARK
Brussels

Not many people know about the air-raid bunker hidden deep below the Parc de Bruxelles (*Warandepark*). Constructed in 1938 to protect the country's political leaders, it was later used by the Nazis and then converted into a nuclear bunker during the Cold War. Look behind the Cercle Gaulois building and you will spot steps under the green trellis leading down into the bunker, as well as several concrete ventilation shafts.

66 NAMUR CITADEL TUNNELS

NAMUR CITADEL
Route Merveilleuse 64
Namur
+32 (0)81 24 73 70
citadelle.namur.be

Located high above the River Meuse, Namur citadel is one of the most fascinating military complexes in Europe. You can wander above ground through a baffling maze of earthworks, bastions and barracks, but the most impressive fortifications lie deep below ground.

Most of the tunnels are closed off, but there is one place where you can walk through a secret passage inside a 17th-century bastion. The entrance signed Galerie Boileau leads into a damp, dripping passage lined with narrow loophole windows, each with a horizontal iron bar to rest the gun.

67 KEMMEL COMMAND BUNKER

Lettingstraat 64
Kemmel
West Flanders
TICKETS AT:
Sint-Laurentius-plein 1
Kemmel
+32 (0)57 45 04 55
toerismeheuvelland.be

For several decades, no one knew about the Nato bunker buried below the Kemmelberg hill. This vast underground complex was constructed as a command centre for Nato air forces in the event of nuclear war. Abandoned in 1995, it opened to the public in 2010. It's like a James Bond movie set, with military maps on the walls, austere metal cabinets and rows of old telephones from the 1950s, while above ground there is nothing apart from a fake farmhouse hidden in the woods. Tickets have to be bought in advance at Heuvelland tourist office.

68 ST REMACLUS CAVE

Auby-sur-Semois
Luxembourg

The St Remaclus Cave is hidden deep in the Ardennes. You follow a forest trail near the village of Auby-sur-Semois, looking out for the word *Grottes* (caves) painted on trees in faded yellow letters, then pick your way carefully along a narrow ledge high above the River Semois. Eventually you come to a Gothic arch cut out of the crumbling shale rock. It leads into a dark cave with a white limestone statue of St Remaclus tending two sick animals. According to a local legend, the hermit lived here in the 7th century. Many pilgrims have visited the caves over the centuries, including King Albert I who came here as a boy. A few burnt-out candles on the altar prove that people still come to this lonely spot looking for help.

69 KANNE CAVES

Avergat 14
Kanne
Limburg

The strange limestone hills around Kanne village have been quarried for building material since the Middle Ages. The mellow golden stone known locally as *mergel* has been used to build farms, houses and churches along the Meuse valley. The Kanne quarry is no longer worked, leaving behind a network of underground caves used for mushroom cultivation and candlelit wedding receptions. There is even a cycle route through the caves.

70 COUDENBERG

ENTRANCE:
MUSÉE BELVUE
Place des Palais 7
Brussels
+32 (0)2 500 45 54
coudenberg.brussels

For several centuries, the foundations of the Coudenberg Palace lay buried below the cobbles on Place Royale in Brussels. But finally the city restored the ruins to create a unique underground museum. You explore the spotlit mediaeval spaces through a complex route of narrow passages and steep stairs. Along the way, you come across a buried street, a hidden mansion and the shattered stone paving of the great hall.

69 KANNE CAVES

LIÈGE-GUILLEMINS

BUILDINGS

Exceptional ARCHITECTURE

71 WINTER GARDEN IN THE URSULINE CONVENT

Bosstraat 9
Onze-Lieve-Vrouw-Waver
Antwerp
+32 (0)15 75 77 28
visitwintertuin.be

The winter garden of the Ursuline Convent is one of the most beautiful art nouveau buildings in the country. The only problem is it is hidden inside a Catholic convent school. It used to be almost impossible to visit, but now you can book to join a guided tour on Sunday afternoons.
The winter garden was designed to impress wealthy parents who were looking for a good boarding school for their daughters. It is a stunning art nouveau space with a vaulted iron roof, stained glass windows and palm trees in pots. The guided tour takes in other surprising spaces, including empire-style interiors, galleries with tiled floors, and a beautiful corridor lined with 35 neat little rooms where girls sat at pianos practising their pieces.

72 PALACE OF THE PRINCE-BISHOPS

Place Saint-Lambert 18
Liège

It can look forbidding from the outside. You have to squeeze past a barrier to enter the courtyard. Sometimes armed police block the entrance because the building is now occupied by law courts. But it was originally a palace built in the 16th century in the early renaissance style of Italy. The courtyard is surrounded by an arcade with columns decorated in grotesque style.

The bizarre faces, monsters and vegetation add to the menacing atmosphere of the courts. Look carefully in the arcade near the entrance and you will find a bronze plaque embossed with the last letter Georges Simenon wrote before he died.

73 ROYAL LODGE, GROENENDAAL

O.L.V. van Loretopad (near Groenendaal station) Hoeilaart Flemish Brabant

A strange forgotten pavilion stands deep in the forest to the south of Brussels. It was built by King Albert I in 1924 as a royal lodge overlooking the Groenendaal racecourse. The racecourse had been founded 35 years earlier by his predecessor. Once the haunt of European high society, it had its own railway station, elegant wrought iron grandstands and betting shops. But it closed in 1991, leaving just the isolated royal lodge, which was restored in 2016 as a venue for weddings and meetings.
You can track down a training racecourse hidden in the woods to the north. Enclosed by earth embankments, this course is still used by horse riders.

74 VAUX-HALL

PARC DE BRUXELLES / WARANDEPARK
Brussels
vauxhallsummer.brussels

A narrow cobbled lane next to the Théâtre du Parc in Brussels leads to the forgotten Vaux-Hall. Hidden among tall trees, this intriguing neoclassical building was constructed on the edge of the park in the 18th century. Inspired by the Vauxhall Pleasure Gardens in London, it served at different times as a concert hall, ballroom and cafe. The annual festival Vaux-Hall Summer was launched here in 2018 featuring concerts, films, dance and children's activities.

Walk around to the back of the building and you will see a curious green lattice arcade built around the courtyard. This was begun in 1913, along with the elegant music kiosk, but not completed until 1921. The kiosk was eventually taken over as a private residence, while the delicate arcade gradually rotted away. Finally, the city brought in skilled craftsmen from the Vosges region of France to restore the wood and metal structure. Completed in 2017, the arcade is occasionally used for concerts or film screenings in the summer. But it is normally deserted.

75 THE OLD CITY

OPEN-AIR MUSEUM BOKRIJK

Bokrijklaan 1
Genk
Limburg
+32 (0)11 26 53 00
bokrijk.be

Created in the 1950s, Bokrijk open-air museum offers a nostalgic glimpse of Flemish village life. Located in rural Limburg, the museum brings together dozens of reconstructed buildings including farmhouses, a chapel and a windmill, along with several village inns where you can drink a local beer.

But there is one strange area almost no one discovers called 'De Oude Stad' (The Old City). Here you find 17 historic buildings that stood in Antwerp until the 1960s. This reconstructed urban district was never particularly popular with visitors, so the museum came up with a plan to turn it into a sixties experience. Now there is an Esso garage squeezed next to old brick houses, along with an early supermarket and a 1960s bar. It makes no sense.

76 SQUARE COGHEN

Square Coghen
Uccle
Brussels

This hidden enclave of art deco and modernist houses lies off Avenue Brugmann. It dates from 1929 when Belgian architects were experimenting with bold new forms of construction. Some of the houses have interesting details such as round porthole windows, jagged profiles and curved balconies. But few people ever discover this forgotten corner of Uccle, where the architecture harks back to a lost golden age of jazz music and ocean liners.

77 CITÉ MIROIR

Place Xavier-Neujean 22
Liège
+32 (0)4 230 70 50
citemiroir.be

An ambitious project has transformed a modernist swimming pool in the heart of Liège into a cultural centre. The original pool was located at the top of the building with huge glass windows looking out on the old town. This impressive space, which reopened in 2014, is now used for temporary exhibitions. The centre also incorporates a socialist library and a cafe.

78 DE NOTELAER

Notelaerdreef 2
Hingene
Antwerp
+32 (0)3 889 69 20
notelaer.be

The d'Ursel family once organised parties and feasts in a hunting lodge looking out on the River Scheldt. The elegant octagonal building was designed by a French architect in the style of an Italian belvedere. The salon on the first floor was decorated with beautiful parquet floor and reliefs illustrating mythological scenes.

During the North Sea storm of 1953, the River Scheldt flooded the little pavilion behind the dike. The building was rescued by the Belgian artist Vic Gentils, who turned it into a studio. The pavilion is now a protected monument with a cafe on the ground floor and a small museum above.

79 LUCAS HUYS

Minderbroeders-straat 10
Bruges
West Flanders

The black wooden mansion facing the Astridpark in Bruges is something of a mystery. Dated 1573 on a small stone tablet, it looks authentic enough, but it is actually made from fragments of other buildings. Local historians claim the wooden façade originally stood somewhere in Brussels, but no one in the Brussels city archives can confirm this. It was apparently brought to Bruges in 1889, where it was incorporated into a house designed by Louis Delacenserie. The little spy mirror attached to the wall adds a sinister touch to a building no one really understands.

Dream CASTLES

80 SENEFFE

Rue Lucien
Plasman 7
Seneffe
Hainaut
+32 (0)64 55 69 13
chateaudeseneffe.be

The beautiful bluestone Château de Seneffe lies at the end of a long drive in a forgotten corner of Belgium. It is not too well known, yet this is one of the most intriguing castles in the country.

It was built in the 18th century by a wealthy arms dealer from Brussels. The nouveau riche owner set out to impress his visitors with a classical château, formal gardens and Palladian theatre. Abandoned in the 20th century, the building came close to being demolished, but was eventually restored by the Belgian government as a museum of silverware.

The intimate interiors on the ground floor were recently redesigned to evoke the intellectual and sensual mood of the Enlightenment. After slipping on shoe covers to protect the parquet, you can wander through the rooms experiencing the sounds, smells and fabrics of the 18th century. It is an astonishingly rich and erotic experience, inspired by rococo paintings and the novel *Les Liaisons Dangereuses*.

You can also watch a film inspired by old scientific experiments, eat lunch in the former orangery and listen to philosophical discussions in the little theatre in the garden. But perhaps the most decadent moment comes on Saturday and Sunday afternoons when visitors can drink hot chocolate from a silver pot in a quaint Chinese salon.

81 FREŸR

Freyr 12
Hastière
Namur
+32 (0)82 22 22 00
freyr.be

This spectacular castle stands on the banks of the River Meuse opposite the sheer Freyr cliffs. Built in the 1570s, the castle embodies the mellow brick and stone style of the Meuse Renaissance. Freÿr is famous for the pleasure gardens planted more than two centuries later in formal French style with ponds, a labyrinth and fountains. But the finest feature is a neoclassical orangerie built to shelter orange trees purchased from the King of Poland more than 300 years ago. Every summer, the ancient trees are carried out into the garden where they fill the air with the scent of blossom.

82 D'URSEL

Wolfgang d'Urselstraat 9
Hingene
Antwerp
+32 (0)3 820 60 10
kasteeldursel.be

This elegant summer residence is full of secret messages. They were written on the walls by the calligrapher Brody Neuenschwander in 2007, but now lie hidden beneath the delicate wall fabrics. The idea emerged during renovation work in 2016 when decorators discovered inscriptions and collages hidden beneath the old wall fabrics. They were written on the wall in French by two young aristocratic women, Sophie and Juliette, who were staying here in the summer of 1877. "As long as this beloved castle is standing," they wrote, "where so many generations have been happy, we will bless these rooms with our shadows."
Now owned by the Flemish government, the castle decided to copy the idea by inviting the public to send in messages to go on the walls. A local priest wrote a long sermon, a seven-year-old girl sent a letter to Father Christmas and a young couple asked for their initials to be inscribed for ever on the wall.

The messages are now hidden under the new wall fabrics, but they will be revealed at some time in the future. Meanwhile, the castle is funding further renovations by brewing its own beers with honey from the castle's beehives and oak from local woods.

83 REINHARDSTEIN

Chemin du
Cheneux 50
Ovifat
Liège
+32 (0)80 44 68 68
reinhardstein.net

Reinhardstein had been a desolate ruin for 150 years when Brussels historian Jean Overloop stumbled upon it in 1965. Working with local craftsmen, he carefully restored the grim stone fortress and furnished the interior in atmospheric mediaeval style with tapestries, oak chests and armour. Perched high on a rocky outcrop above a misty valley, its foundations date back to 1354. Owned for three centuries by the Metternich family, it was finally abandoned in the early 19th century. Now restored to its old state, it is reached from Robertville reservoir along a dark forest trail. You can visit the interior on a one-hour guided tour and then drink a local Reinhardstein beer in a rustic wooden chalet.

Striking STATIONS

84 ANTWERP DAM STATION

Damplein
Antwerp

You might not think Antwerpen-Dam looks different from any other Belgian station. Located near Park Spoor Noord, it's a typical Flemish Renaissance brick building standing alongside a railway viaduct. But an exhibition of old photographs in the tunnel under the viaduct tells an astonishing story. They reveal the entire station was moved 36 metres in 1907 to make space for a new railway line. The work was done using an ingenious system of mechanical jacks and rails. The company in charge of this exceptional engineering project hoped it could sell the technology elsewhere, but the concept never took off, leaving Dam station as a unique experiment.

85 LIÈGE-GUILLEMINS

Place des Guillemins 2
Liège

Liège was until recently an old industrial city few tourists would dream of visiting. But the city began to change in 2009 with the opening of a sleek new station designed by the Spanish architect Santiago Calatrava. It's an astonishing futuristic building with a swooping steel and glass canopy poised above the tracks like a gigantic wave. Now it is worth travelling to Liège just to admire the architecture. Start at the top level, high above the trains, where you can admire a neighbourhood slowly emerging from urban decline. Then go down to the ground floor where cafes and ticket offices occupy

curious round glass pods. The station neighbourhood is still far from finished, but one day you will be able to walk into town along a magnificent waterfront promenade.

86 DE HAAN TRAM STATION

Nieuwe Rijksweg 1
De Haan
West Flanders

The tram pulls up in De Haan next to a beautiful art nouveau station built in 1888. It was designed by the Brussels architect G. Dhaeyer in a fanciful style with steep overhanging eaves, elegant carved wood and the French name Coq-sur-Mer in decorative letters. A sign recalls that Albert Einstein stepped off the tram here in 1933 at the start of his exile at the coast.

87 RONSE STATION

West Churchill-plein 6
Ronse
East Flanders

The oldest surviving railway station in mainland Europe stands near the language border in Ronse/Renaix. But it wasn't always here. It was built by a Brussels architect in 1841-48 on 't Zand square in Bruges. Eventually the classical building became too small to cope with the tourists visiting Bruges. A new Gothic station was constructed in 1881 and the old station was rebuilt in Ronse/Renaix.

88 GHOST STATIONS ON THE NORTH-SOUTH LINE

BRUXELLES-CHAPELLE
Rue des Ursulines

BRUXELLES-CONGRÈS
(closed at weekends)
Av Pacheco 25
Brussels

The busy rail tunnel running through Brussels has five official stations but most trains only stop at three. To cut journey times, most trains ignore Bruxelles-Chapelle and Bruxelles-Congrès. These deserted underground stations are like the creepy abandoned stations in East Berlin during the Cold War. The Chapelle station in the Marolles district was until recently occupied by a cultural centre, but is currently abandoned.

The other station, Bruxelles-Congrès, is harder to find. You might spot the huge ventilation tower dating from the period when steam trains passed through the tunnel. It's worth going down the steps to admire the modernist interior which has barely changed since the station opened in 1952. You can still see the polished wood panelling, ticket office and abandoned station bar. But it is strangely silent, apart from the gentle vibration of a passing train.

Peculiar CHURCHES

89 READING BETWEEN THE LINES

Grootloonstraat 2
Borgloon
Limburg

You have to hike through apple orchards near Borgloon to reach the strange transparent church called *Reading between the Lines*. Designed in 2011 by experimental Belgian architects Pieterjan Gijs and Arnout Van Vaerenbergh, it sits on a hill with a sweeping view across the lush landscape. Modelled on local churches in the region, the installation is made from horizontal steel plates that almost disappear when the building is seen from certain angles. The visual confusion continues when you stand inside the church looking out at the landscape. It's a strangely poetic spot where local

89 READING BETWEEN THE LINES

people sometimes gather in the evening to watch the sun go down.
Located between cycle points 154 and 155. A walking trail runs from the Markt square in Borgloon to the *Doorkijkkerk* (Transparent Church).

90 OOSTERWEEL CHURCH

Kastelweg
Antwerp

An abandoned and overgrown church in Antwerp's port area is all that survives of the lost village of Oosterweel. Hidden from view in a sunken area of woodland, the mediaeval church can only be reached by scrambling down a muddy embankment. The 13th-century village of Oosterweel once had more than one thousand inhabitants. It gave its name to a sea battle fought in 1567 at the start of the Eighty Years' War. But the village disappeared in 1958 when the port expanded, leaving just this forgotten church, lost in the middle of a vast industrial zone. Located near cycle point 55.

91 OLD HOSPITAL CHAPEL

Budastraat 37
Kortrijk
West Flanders

A forgotten baroque chapel stands on an island in Kortrijk next to an ancient hospital. This tiny historic chapel is reached down a long, dusty cloister. The interior contains old paintings, statues and marble tombs of former sisters. A curious statue to the left of the altar shows the obscure Saint Donatus who is said to protect against lightning.

92 AMUZ FOYER

Kammenstraat 81
Antwerp
+32 (0)3 202 46 69
amuz.be

A mysterious little chapel lies off the trendy Kammenstraat in central Antwerp. Built in 1857 in neo-Byzantine style, it was used in winter for services when the larger baroque church next door became too cold.

92 **AMUZ FOYER**

The startling interior is decorated with colourful murals and stained glass. The main church has now been converted into a concert hall (with modern underfloor heating), while Sunday brunch is served in the winter chapel.

93 CANADIAN CHAPEL

Avenue de la Vecquée
Malonne
Namur

A strange painted wooden chapel stands next to the main road in the village of Malonne. Known as the Canadian chapel, it was built by a local aristocrat. Abandoned for many years, it is now used by the local Russian community for Orthodox services.

94 LOUISE-MARIE CHAPEL

Petrus en Paulusplein
Ostend
West Flanders

Ostend's dark neo-Gothic church contains a beautiful chapel hidden behind the altar with a sad marble monument dedicated to Queen Louise-Marie. She died in Ostend at the age of 38 in a house now occupied by the city museum. The statue shows the dying queen gazing up at an angel while a weeping woman symbolising the people of Ostend sits at her feet.

95 WEAVERS' CHAPEL

Kortedagsteeg 12
Ghent
East Flanders

It's easy to walk past the beautiful weavers' chapel in Ghent. It looks like an ordinary shopfront until you step through the door. You suddenly find yourself inside a 14th-century chapel with whitewashed walls and a high vaulted roof. Originally built for the Guild of Weavers, the chapel has been used in the past as a cinema, reading room and garage. Converted into a retail space in 2002 by the Antwerp architect Christine Conix, it is currently occupied by the Danish design store Bolia.

Remarkable BRIDGES

96 PONT DE CLAIES

Vresse-sur-Semois
Namur

A temporary footbridge called the Pont de Claies is constructed every summer at a quiet spot on the River Semois near the village of Vresse-sur-Semois. It is the last surviving example of a traditional hurdle bridge built out of wooden posts supporting a wicker deck. These bridges originally allowed workers to reach the tobacco fields along the river. Once the bridge has been constructed, you can cross the Semois to the beautiful village of Laforêt. But it only survives a couple of months. By early September, nothing remains except a little sign on a tree to say the bridge has been dismantled.

97 ROMAN BRIDGE

Rue du Pont
Romain
Erquelinnes
Hainaut

It isn't Roman and it isn't really a bridge, but it is called the *pont romain*. Located in a quiet wooded valley close to the French border, the bridge crosses the little River Hantes on 13 stone arches. It stands close to the ancient Roman road from Trier to Bavai, but was built in the Middle Ages as a barrage. Repaired many times over the centuries, it is now closed to traffic. A shrine to the Virgin Mary stands in a little grotto nearby. Covered with teddy bears and urgent prayers, it adds to the mystery of this strange spot.

98 LA BELLE LIÉGEOISE

PARC DE LA BOVERIE

Boulevard Frère-Orban 180
Liège

A new steel footbridge with a timber deck sweeps across the Meuse to connect Liège-Guillemins station with the Parc de la Boverie. Built in 2016, it is named La Belle Liégeoise after an 18th-century woman called Anne-Josèphe de Méricourt who played a leading role in the French Revolution, dressing as a man while calling for women's rights.

99 GENK CYCLE BRIDGE

Kuilenstraat/
Westerring
Genk
Limburg

A striking cycle bridge crosses the busy Westerring (West ring road) in Genk in a series of gentle loops. The white steel structure, which looks like a roller coaster, was constructed in 2014 to connect two districts separated by a busy four-lane highway. Located between cycle points 560 and 29.

100 LICHTENLIJN FOOTBRIDGE

Elisabethlaan
(On the municipal border between Knokke and Zeebrugge)
Knokke
West Flanders

The Brussels engineering firm Ney & Partners built a beautiful swooping steel bridge in Knokke in 2008. Inspired by the shape of a hammock, it carries cyclists and pedestrians across a busy coastal road separating the beach from the inland polders. Located between cycle points 36 and 38.

101 COLLEGEBRUG

Diksmuidekaai/
IJzerkaai
Kortrijk
West Flanders

Kortrijk is building seven new bridges over the River Leie as part of a bold plan to revitalise the city's historic waterfront. The most striking is the shiny steel Collegebrug designed by architects SumProject to carry cyclists and walkers over the river in a series of sensual curves. The architects also created a park next to the bridge on the IJzerkaai called Buda Beach where a summer cafe spreads out along the waterfront.

101 COLLEGEBRUG

Modern **BUILDINGS**

102 ATELIER JESPERS

Avenue du Prince Héritier 149
Woluwe-Saint-Lambert
Brussels
atelierjespers.com

The modernist architect Victor Bourgeois built this white building in 1928 as a house and studio for the expressionist sculptor Oscar Jespers. The striking curved front sparked off a furious reaction in this quiet bourgeois neighbourhood. But it became a meeting place for Europe's avant-garde artists such as Kandinsky and Klee, and passed through various owners after Jespers died in 1970. In 2016 it was bought by an art collector who opened it to the public as a gallery, so it is now sometimes possible to get inside one of the most stunning architectural spaces in Belgium.

103 GUIETTE HOUSE

Populierenlaan 32
Antwerp

A striking white house designed by the French architect Le Corbusier stands out from its neighbours in a quiet Antwerp suburb. Built in 1926 as a private home and studio for the modern artist René Guiette, it is one of Le Corbusier's early works. The design is based on Le Corbusier's innovative idea of the Maison Citrohan – an efficient modern house modelled on a mass-produced Citroën car. Restored in 1988, the house is one of just 17 buildings by Le Corbusier listed as UNESCO world heritage.

104 LA MAISON DE VERRE

Rue Lejeune
Uccle
Brussels

Brussels promotes its art nouveau architecture, but forgets all the other styles that can be found in the city. La Maison de Verre gets little attention, yet it is an exceptional example of the modernist style that emerged in Europe in the 1930s. Designed by the young architect Paul-Amaury Michel in 1935 as his own home, it was inspired by Le Corbusier's ideas as well as the Rietveld Schroder House in Utrecht.

105 ST RITA'S CHURCH

J. Sabbestraat 43
Harelbeke
West Flanders

One of the most extraordinary buildings in Belgium is located in the quiet town of Harelbeke, just outside Kortrijk. Begun in 1963, St Rita's Church is dedicated to the patron saint of impossible causes. And this church does look as if it should not exist. It was designed by Léon Stynen and Paul Demeyer in a bold brutalist style inspired by Le Corbusier. It took three years to construct the striking concrete structure, which rises above the surrounding houses like a huge tent. The austere interior is illuminated by a shaft of light that streams through a large round window in the roof.

106 MUSÉE L

Place des Sciences 3
Louvain-la-Neuve
Walloon Brabant
+32 (0)10 47 48 41
museel.be

A strange brutalist building stands on the main square in the university town of Louvain-la-Neuve. Designed by the architect André Jacqmain in 1970, the building was planned as a science library at the heart of the utopian new town. The interior spaces are crafted out of raw concrete moulded into mysterious, sensual curves. Recently restored to its original state, it opened in late 2017 as a museum dedicated to art and science.

107 LA COUR SAINT-ANTOINE

Rue Hors-Château 114
Liège

You could easily walk straight past it. Two classical columns mark the entrance to a secret courtyard in the heart of Liège that was once an abandoned back yard filled with old junk. The architect Charles Vandenhove restored the courtyard in 1979 to create an almost Italian square. He also renovated the 17th-century houses and added little details of his own including classical columns, tiles in the style of Charles Rennie Mackintosh and a pink postmodern temple. The French artists Anne and Patrick Poirier later added a curious fountain and a stream called *Tikal* inspired by Mayan temples.

Obscure INTERIORS

108 HOFKAMER

Oude Beurs 27
Antwerp
+32 (0)3 226 31 85
openmonumenten.be/monumenten/den-wolsack-en-de-hofkamer

The curious 18th-century Hofkamer lies hidden behind the grand Antwerp mansion Den Wolsack. Forgotten for many years, this remarkable interior was finally revealed to the public in 2017. Reached through a courtyard, the Hofkamer has a large ballroom on the ground floor with a huge painted ceiling illustrating *The Gods on Mount Olympus*. A spiral staircase leads up to a room decorated with contemporary art by Koen van den Broek. But the strangest space is a curious bookcase toilet lined with fake volumes made from leather and wood. Open on Wednesday and Saturday afternoon.

109 HOTEL D'HANE-STEENHUYSE

Veldstraat 55
Ghent
East Flanders
+32 (0)9 266 85 00
historischehuizen.stad.gent

Located on the narrow Veldstraat in Ghent, this gorgeous rococo palace takes its name from the d'Hane de Steenhuyse family. It was occupied in 1815 by King Louis XVIII of France during the 'Hundred Days' when Napoleon seized power. It is now an empty, forgotten building, rarely open to the public. But you can sometimes explore the echoing interior to see the dining room where Louis ate supper while locals peered through the windows, and the glittering ballroom where the exiled king entertained British officers before they marched off to Waterloo. Visits on Friday, Saturday and Sunday.

110 WOLFERS SHOP INTERIOR

ART & HISTORY MUSEUM

Cinquantenaire Park
Brussels
+32 (0)2 741 73 02
kmkg-mrah.be

A stunning art nouveau shop interior has been reconstructed inside the Art & History Museum in Brussels. Victor Horta designed the interior in 1912 for the Wolfers jewellery shop. He created the counters and cabinets out of expensive black marble and rare Cuban wood. When the store closed down, its dazzling interior was saved. It went on show for the first time in late 2017.

Inspiring

NEW ARCHITECTURE

111 **PORT HOUSE**
Zaha Hadidplein 1
Antwerp
+32 (0)3 205 20 11
portofantwerp.com

Antwerp Port Authority occupies a stunning building in the industrial docklands to the north of the old town. Located on a remote waterfront site, it is not particularly easy to reach, but it is worth the trip, especially on a weekday when the huge inner courtyard is open to the public.
The building was originally a 20th-century fire station modelled on a 16th-century Renaissance

111 PORT HOUSE

building owned by the Hanseatic League. Shortly before her death in 2016, the British architect Zaha Hadid transformed the fire station by adding a glass structure perched on the roof like a ship. Once inside the courtyard, you can admire the massive steel struts supporting the glass superstructure. Embedded in the floor is an enormous aerial photograph of Antwerp port, along with three anamorphic paintings by Italian street artist Vera Bugatti.
Located near cycle point 54.

112 DE KROOK

M. Makebaplein 1
Ghent
East Flanders
+32 (0)9 323 68 00
dekrook.be

The new Ghent city library is a sleek building of black steel and glass located on a bend in the Schelde known as De Waalse Krook. Designed by local architects Coussée & Goris working with the Catalan firm RCR Arquitectes, the library is a quiet, understated building in a neglected urban neighbourhood. The architects have created some striking interior spaces including a viewing room on the third floor where you can sit on armchairs gazing out at the city skyline. They also added terraces around the building where concerts can be organised and a stylish cafe with sober black furniture.

113 **M**

L. Vanderkelen-
straat 28
Leuven
Flemish Brabant
+32 (0)16 27 29 29
mleuven.be

The old cabinet of curiosities once known as Museum Vander Kelen-Mertens is now called M. Simple as that. In 2010 the Ghent architect Stéphane Beel brilliantly transformed the creaky town museum in Leuven into a stunning contemporary art venue. The building incorporates a kids' area, cafe and rooftop terrace. The museum puts on interesting temporary exhibitions as well as displaying paintings and religious sculptures in a series of intriguing spaces where modern works are hung next to Old Masters.

113 M

114 BLUE TOWER

Boulevard Pierre Mayence
Charleroi
Hainaut

The French architect Jean Nouvel was invited to Charleroi to design a new police station in 2014. Working with the Brussels firm MDW Architecture, Nouvel came up with a striking 70-metre blue tower rising above a 19th-century cavalry barracks occupied by the acclaimed dance company Charleroi danse. The neighbourhood is likely to get a further boost when the Fine Arts Museum moves into former cavalry stables on this site.

114 BLUE TOWER

115 TYNE COT VISITORS CENTRE

Vijfwegestraat
Zonnebeke
West Flanders

Tyne Cot Cemetery is the largest British military cemetery in the world, with 12.000 graves and a further 35.000 names of missing soldiers carved on a long wall at the back. As you approach this overwhelming spot, you hear a haunting woman's voice slowly recite the names of the dead. You then enter a simple modern pavilion designed in 2006 by the Bruges architects Govaert & Vanhoutte with a glass wall providing a sweeping view of the former battlefield.

116 EUROPA BUILDING

Rue de la Loi 155
European Quarter
Brussels
+32 (0)2 281 59 20
consilium.europa.eu/en/contact/visits

A striking new building has gone up in Brussels to accommodate the powerful European Council, which brings together the EU's political leaders. Designed by the Belgian architects Samyn and Partners and the Italian Studio Valle Progettazioni, it has a central meeting hall in the shape of a giant egg enclosed in a large cube made from recycled window frames salvaged from demolished buildings across Europe. The building was commissioned by Belgium's former Prime Minister Herman Van Rompuy while he was president of the European Council.

LAEKEN CEMETERY

PLACES

Eccentric COLLECTIONS

117 NATURAL HISTORY MUSEUM, TOURNAI

HÔTEL DE VILLE
Rue St-Martin 52
Tournai
Hainaut
+32 (0)69 33 23 43
mhn.tournai.be

Founded in 1829, one year before the Belgian Revolution, this cabinet of curiosities in Tournai is the oldest museum in Belgium. It occupies a beautiful arcade inside the town hall designed by the architect Bruno Renard. Here you can admire a fascinating collection of animals, including the first elephant to arrive in Belgium, along with rare Egyptian turtles and endangered boa constrictors. The museum was recently restored to preserve its authentic 19th-century atmosphere.

118 BELLE EPOQUE CENTRE

Elisabethstraat 24
Blankenberge
West Flanders
+32 (0)50 63 66 40
belleepoque centrum.be

The beach town of Blankenberge is mostly modern apartments, but there are a few architectural treasures in the quiet back streets. A few blocks from the beach, the Belle Epoque Centre occupies a row of three houses built in the flamboyant style of the late 19th century. The houses are filled with relics from the time when Blankenberge was considered the most elegant resort on the North Sea. Visitors can enter a living room furnished in period style, listen to music hall songs on headphones and step out onto an astonishing roof terrace with a replica Gaudí bench made using ceramic tiles salvaged from demolished seaside houses.

119 MUSEUM DR. GUISLAIN

J. Guislainstraat 43
Ghent
East Flanders
+32 (0)9 398 69 50
museumdrguislain.be

The strange and haunting Dr. Guislain Museum occupies one wing of a model psychiatric institution founded in the 19th century by Dr. Jozef Guislain. Visitors can wander through chilling deserted wards still furnished with iron beds and old medical equipment. One room contains a terrifying mechanical saw used in operations to remove the top of the skull. The temporary exhibitions are always fascinating, as is the extensive collection of outsider art. Almost no one leaves this museum untouched.

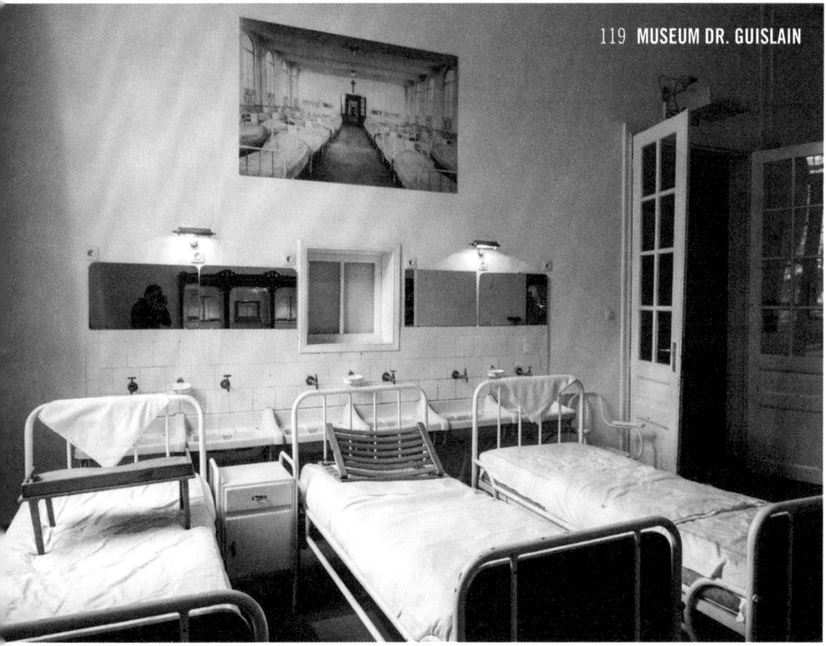
119 MUSEUM DR. GUISLAIN

120 STADSMUSEUM OOSTENDE

Langestraat 69
Ostend
West Flanders
+32 (0)59 51 67 21
oostende.be/stadsmuseum

The fascinating Ostend City Museum moved a few years ago into the former summer residence of the Belgian royal family. The grand, slightly shabby rooms are filled with an eclectic collection of Ostend curiosities gathered by the local history society, including music boxes, ship models, sea charts, souvenirs and ferry timetables. Highlights include a reconstructed fisherman's tavern and a frieze commemorating the Siege of Ostend. The museum also has some mementoes of Queen Louise-Marie, the first Belgian queen, who died in this building. A creaking staircase leads to the top of the building where a little observatory was built for the queen. When she became too sick to climb the steps, she was hoisted up here on a chair to enjoy the sea view.

121 HÔPITAL NOTRE-DAME À LA ROSE

Place Alix de Rosoit
Lessines
Hainaut
+32 (0)68 33 24 03
notredamealarose.be

Lessines is an old Walloon town with some impressive industrial ruins along the banks of the River Dendre. It's not a place tourists normally visit, yet it has an extraordinary building hidden behind a high wall. One of the oldest hospitals in Europe, Notre-Dame à la Rose was founded in 1242. Rebuilt in the 17th century in Flemish Renaissance style, it served as a hospital up until 1980. Today the hospital is a fascinating museum. Wandering through the rooms, you come across reconstructed nun's cells, a historical pharmacy and a furnished hospital ward. The objects on display include medical books, frightening surgical devices and an astonishing painting of a bearded Christ with female breasts. You can also wander through a walled garden, enter a chilly ice cellar and sit on the cafe terrace with a local Helkiase beer from Brasserie Dupont.

Curious FOLLIES

122 GROTTO OF ST ANTHONY

Rue Haute 7
Crupet
Namur

Canon Jules Gérard spent the first three years of the 20th century creating a fantastic folly dedicated to St Anthony of Padua, the patron saint of lost things. Hidden behind the parish church in the tiny Ardennes village of Crupet, the eccentric structure was built out of 300 tons of local stone, cast iron, and concrete. It is decorated with 22 brightly painted statues of humans and animals recreating four scenes from Anthony's life, including a miracle involving a mule and a curious episode when fish listened to Anthony while he preached. But the most bizarre feature is a massive 700-kilo figure of the devil made from solid iron who is shown trying to tempt the saint. The grotto used to attract thousands of pilgrims, but it is now almost forgotten.

123 EBEN-EZER TOWER

Haie de Wonck
Eben-Emael
Liège
+32 (0)4 286 92 79
musee-du-silex.be

A rough track leads up to an enigmatic flint tower above the village of Bassenge. Even before you arrive, you notice four enormous biblical animals on the roof. This eccentric tower was built in the 1960s by local quarry worker Robert Garcet using discarded rubble. He based the design on obscure religious ideas and mystical measurements. It now contains a rather forgotten private museum with small rooms on five floors filled with fossils, flint objects, skeletons and photographs. The woods around the tower are dotted with odd sculptures hidden among the trees.

124 ABANDONED BOEING 707

Kwatrechtse-steenweg 114
Wetteren
East Flanders

Not too many people can explain the old Boeing 707 plane perched on the roof of a textile factory near the town of Wetteren. The 1957 aircraft once belonged to the Moonie cult leader Sun Myung Moon, who personalised the interior with a mahogany bed, bathtub with gold taps and private cinema. It was acquired in 1985 by the president of Benin as his personal aircraft, but grounded at Ostend airport in 1990 due to safety concerns. It remained there for five years, leaving the small African country with an enormous bill for unpaid parking charges.

The abandoned and rusting plane finally ended up in the hands of a Belgian politician and businessman who moved it to an abandoned car park near Wetteren. For a time, it was used as a training centre for aircraft cleaners. Eventually the local council told the owner he didn't have planning permission to park his aircraft on the site. He called the decision 'childish and petty' and hired two giant cranes to lift the plane onto the factory roof. It is still there.

125 THIÉRY WING

Halfmaartstraat
Leuven
Flemish Brabant

A curious row of houses is hidden behind the Sint-Gertrudiskerk in the university town of Leuven. They were built using rubble salvaged from buildings destroyed by the German army in 1914. This unusual project was proposed by Armand Thiéry, a professor who sat on the committee for the reconstruction of Leuven. He came up with the idea of using old masonry salvaged from houses built in the 17th and 18th centuries. This architectural oddity was converted into apartments in the 1980s.

126 DE NORMANDIE

Koninklijke Baan 1
Koksijde
West Flanders
+32 (0)58 51 81 41
denormandie.be

You pass some strange and beautiful places on the coast tram. But possibly the strangest building can be spotted just outside Koksijde. Built in 1935, it was modelled on the glamorous transatlantic liner De Normandie. It has two funnels, a deck and a row of portholes. But it is made of concrete. The stranded ship is now a restaurant where you can eat *tomate crevettes* made with shrimps caught by horseback fishermen off the beach in Oostduinkerke.

Small and unusual **MUSEUMS**

127 MUNDANEUM

Rue de Nimy 76
Mons
Hainaut
+32 (0)65 31 53 43
mundaneum.org

Belgium has many strange collections, but the Mundaneum is maybe the oddest. Located in an abandoned department store in the southern Belgian town of Mons, it contains a vast collection of newspapers, index cards, posters, tickets, catalogues and curiosities of all sorts. The collection was begun in the early 20th century by the idealists Paul Otlet and Henri La Fontaine, who aimed to gather together all the world's knowledge in a single collection. As well as filling several buildings with anything he could find, Otlet invented the library index card to impose order and tried to develop a special telescope so people could access documents remotely. The project ran into financial problems in the 1930s and the vast collection of documents ended up dumped in a Brussels underground car park. It was almost destroyed, but in 1998 the flamboyant Mons mayor Elio Di Rupo stepped in to save the collection. It was rehoused in an old department store and, with funding from Google, rebranded as the world's first internet. The impressive main hall is filled with rows of old wooden filing cabinets along with photographs, plans and letters. Other rooms are devoted to temporary exhibitions.

128 MUSÉE DES BEAUX-ARTS, TOURNAI

Enclos Saint-Martin 3
Tournai
Hainaut
+32 (0)69 33 24 31
mba.tournai.be

The sleepy town of Tournai doesn't get too many tourists, yet it has a stunning museum in an art deco building designed by Victor Horta. The museum opened in 1928 to display a private collection of 300 paintings acquired by the Belgian hotel owner Henri Van Cutsem. He originally planned to leave the collection to the Belgian state, but the ungrateful government refused the collection because it contained the nude painting *Périmèle, nymph of Capri*. Van Cutsem then commissioned his friend Horta to design a museum in Tournai. It displays some remarkable works, including Manet's lovely *Argenteuil* painted on the banks of the Seine in the summer of 1874.

129 'T GASTHUYS MUSEUM

Oude Vismarkt 13
Aalst
East Flanders
+32 (0)53 72 36 02
tgasthuys.be

The city museum of Aalst occupies a beautiful former hospice known as 't Gasthuys. The mediaeval building has been sensitively restored with whitewashed walls, tiled floors and a walled herb garden. It feels like a calm, contemplative place. But all hell breaks loose on the first floor where two large rooms are dedicated to Aalst's Carnival celebrations. Here you are surrounded by masks, costumes and mad scenes. One section is dedicated to the 'Voil Jeanetten' and their ridiculous prams, fake breasts and bird cages. Another room is filled with photographs that evoke the three days of chaos before Lent.
The peaceful mood of the old hospice is restored in a quiet upstairs room dedicated to the 20th-century Aalst painter Valerius De Saedeleer. The walls are lined with subtle, mystical paintings of the Flemish landscape that could almost have been done by Bruegel.

130 TESEUM

Museumkwartier 2
Tongeren
Limburg
+32 (0)12 80 02 28
teseum.be

An astonishing underground museum in Tongeren reveals Roman remains discovered by archaeologists when they dug down under the Gothic basilica. The site includes the foundations of a bath house and traces of two Roman houses, as well as pottery shards, fragments of wall paintings and animal bones.
Designed by a team of historians, designers, musicians and IT engineers, the museum offers a headphone-guided route through the dark underground spaces. The tour ends dramatically inside the foundations of a vanished Roman villa where you see the charred remains of a beam set on fire during the destruction of Tongeren in 275 AD. With the background sound of the burning city in your headphones, the cracked brick walls and blackened wood bring you close to the moment the Roman Empire died.

131 VAN BUUREN MUSEUM

Avenue
Léo Errera 41
Uccle
Brussels
+32 (0)2 343 48 51
museumvanbuuren.be

The art deco house built by David and Alice Van Buuren is one of the most poetic spots in Brussels. Hidden away in a quiet suburb, the brick house was designed in 1928 in Amsterdam School style for a wealthy Dutch banker and his wife. They furnished the interior in a luxurious art deco style and built up an exceptional art collection, including a painting hanging in the staircase by the Flemish artist Gustave Van de Woestijne showing five fair-haired Flemish children sitting down to lunch. There is more to discover out in the garden where the landscape gardeners Jules Buyssens and later René Pechère created gorgeous little gardens, including a *Garden of the Heart* created by Alice in memory of her husband.

132 MU.ZEE

Romestraat 11
Ostend
West Flanders
+32 (0)59 50 81 18
muzee.be

The museum of contemporary art in Ostend is located in a modernist building once occupied by a cooperative department store. Displayed in calm white spaces, the collection includes works by Permeke, Ensor, Spilliaert and Broodthaers. But it also has raw new art by Belgian artists such as Jan Vercruysse and Jacqueline Mesmaeker.

132 MU.ZEE

133 **PLASTER CAST WORKSHOP**

CINQUANTENAIRE PARK

Brussels

+32 (0)2 741 72 94

kmkg-mrah.be

Hidden at the back of the Art & History Museum in Brussels, the plaster cast workshop is a fabulous, romantic storeroom and atelier dating back to the 19th century. The workshop was originally founded by the controversial King Leopold II to create replicas of classical sculptures to decorate private mansions, museums and art academies. The vast storage area is filled with rows of wooden shelves piled high with 4000 plaster cast moulds. They can be used to create plaster replicas of anything from a bust of Beethoven to a tiny cat from an Egyptian tomb. The craftsmen work at dusty wooden desks in a workshop dominated by a reproduction of Michelangelo's David. They are happy to explain their work to visitors, while finished replicas are sold in the shop. Open Tuesday to Friday.

Strange VILLAGES

134 **DOEL**
East Flanders

It is almost a ghost town, but Doel still has about 20 residents. It can't be easy living there. This deserted village north of Antwerp, which once had 1300 inhabitants, stands on the banks of the River Scheldt, next to a nuclear power station. The houses were due to be demolished in the 1960s to allow the construction of a new dock, but then the plan was put on hold. Most residents have now left, leaving behind abandoned houses, an empty church and a little harbour. The village has become a favourite location for street artists, including ROA and Bué the Warrior. It also attracts a few tourists, photographers and urbanists. Now there is a bold plan to revive the town. No one knows if Doel will still exist in a year, but it feels like a place that does not want to die.

135 **OUD-REKEM**
Limburg

This lovely old Flemish village stands close to the River Maas near the Dutch border. It's an interesting place to wander with a massive castle once occupied by a psychiatric institution, a town gate and a village square shaded by old trees. You can set off from here on a bike trip along the River Maas, ending up back in Oud-Rekem for a local beer in one of the village cafes.

136 WÉRIS

Luxembourg

Wéris is a strange village made up of old stone and half-timbered houses clustered around an ancient church. People are drawn to this lovely spot in the Ardennes by the neolithic standing stones and dolmens out in the countryside around the village. You can follow marked trails through fields of maize that lead to isolated standing stones, such as the impressive Dolmen d'Oppagne, which lies hidden in a hollow surrounded by four old oak trees. Another trail leads through woods to an abandoned quarry and a standing stone called the *Lit du Diable* which is painted white every year to drive away the devil. The information centre Maison des Mégalithes in the village sells a useful map to the sites and there are several good restaurants where you can eat Ardennes food and drink a local craft beer.

137 BUITENLAND

Near Bornem
Antwerp

The quiet, forgotten village of Buitenland is not the easiest place to find. It stands on a narrow road in a bend of the Old Scheldt. It is a modest place with a factory producing wicker baskets. But something seems out of place. Several old buildings look as if they really belong in Antwerp. They were built for the World Fair of 1894 as part of an attraction called Old Antwerp. After the fair ended, most of the buildings were demolished, but a few were rebuilt in Buitenland by a local builder whose family owned the basket factory. The most impressive is a replica of a 16th-century Antwerp mansion called the *Reuzenhuis*, or Giant's House.

138 **KANNE**

Limburg

The village of Kanne stands next to the River Jeker in a landscape of strange limestone hills. With a population of 1200, the 'white village on the Jeker' has a remarkable 464 protected buildings, including houses built with the mellow local stone and a 1647 church modelled on the Church of the Holy Sepulchre in Jerusalem. A plaque on the wall of the Hotel Huize Poswick recalls an unexplained incident on 18 August 1914 when German soldiers shot the mayor's wife and a local lawyer. Now Kanne is a peaceful spot near the Dutch border with several cafés and an ice-cream salon.

138 KANNE

139 REDU

Redu
Luxembourg
redu-villagedulivre.be

The sleepy Ardennes village of Redu was almost dead when the bookseller Noël Anselot came up with a plan. Inspired by the book town Hay-on-Wye in Wales, he persuaded a few Belgian book dealers to settle here back in 1984. Other dealers followed, snapping up the old schoolhouse, a huge barn and an abandoned snail farm. The village, which has just 400 inhabitants, now boasts about 15 specialised bookshops crammed with rare books, posters and prints. It also has several restaurants, cafes and B&Bs, along with a print shop and a farm where you can pick your own raspberries.

140 ELLEZELLES

Ellezelles
Hainaut

Ellezelles looks like an ordinary Belgian village, but it turns out to have some mysterious traditions. It is the scene of a gathering of witches every year and offers visitors a walking route known as Le Sentier de l'Étrange (The Strange Trail). But strangest of all is its claim to be the birthplace of Hercule Poirot, the Belgian detective created by Agatha Christie. A statue attached to a house wall seems to confirm the story, although it is obviously a cheeky lie.

Lost LANES

141 BEGIJNHOF, KORTRIJK

Begijnhofstraat
Kortrijk
West Flanders

The entrance to the Begijnhof is a small gate that leads into a hidden warren of cobbled lanes lined with old whitewashed houses. A statue near the entrance represents Johanna of Constantinople who founded the Begijnhof in 1238.
You find enclosed communities like this in many Flemish and Dutch cities. Sheltered behind high walls, they were protected places, like towns within towns. They were built for single women who belonged to the order of Beguines. Not much is known about this religious order, although a few scholars argue they were radical feminist communes.
The last member of the order died in Kortrijk in 2013. The complex was recently restored to create affordable local housing, but a tiny dwelling next to the gate has been preserved as a small museum. Visitors can peer through the windows to see inside the simple reconstructed rooms.

142 KADETTESTEEGJE

Lane runs next to Maastrichterstraat 38
Hasselt
Limburg

It's easy to miss the little alley Kadettesteegje in Hasselt. This hidden lane off the Maastrichterstraat leads to a secluded square called Kadetjesplein. Here you find yourself in a walled courtyard with old trees, benches where students eat their lunch, several strange sculptures and a Little Free Library attached to a brick wall. The square was picked by locals a few years ago as one of 25 happiest spots in the city.

143 RUELLE CÉSAR

Ruelle César
Mons
Hainaut

The ancient stone steps known as Ruelle César wind up a hillside in the heart of Mons. They lead among old houses and hidden gardens to emerge on a summit where you can look down on the old rooftops of Mons and beyond to the Borinage region where the young artist Van Gogh lived from 1879 to 1880.

144 IMPASSE DE L'ANGE

Impasse de l'Ange
Liège

Liège may look a bit ugly and neglected, but it has some beautiful hidden spots, like the old lanes off the ancient Hors-Château. One of the most intriguing of these passages is the Impasse de l'Ange, which gets its name from the little statue of an angel on a house next to the alley. The narrow alley leads past former workers' houses into a hidden courtyard where residents have created a tiny urban garden filled with abandoned tricycles, rusting barbecue stands and piles of chopped logs. Another lane called Impasse de la Couronne leads into the same courtyard. Someone has placed a bench in the alley with a fake street sign reading *Place des Amoureux*, the Square of the Lovers. Not far away, the narrow alley Impasse Venta runs between high whitewashed walls into a tiny courtyard.

145 **OLIEBAAN**

Oliebaan
Bruges
West Flanders

There are secret streets in Bruges where tourists never walk. The Oliebaan is one of them. It feels as if you have left the overcrowded city behind when you turn down this ancient lane. Squeezed between brown brick walls, it looks as if it leads nowhere. But keep on walking and you come to a muddy field with fruit trees growing next to the city walls and cows grazing on land once owned by Cistercian monks.

145 **OLIEBAAN**

146 RUE ROTURE

Off Rue Puits-en-Sock Liège

A narrow mediaeval passage closed off with an iron barrier leads into an unexpected enclave in the centre of Liège. The narrow cobbled street known as Roture is lined with ancient houses in Meuse Renaissance style. It leads to a charming little square with a tiny Madonna statue and a fountain with four lion heads. Many of the houses have been turned into small theatres, restaurants and bars, turning Roture into a lively nightlife neighbourhood in the heart of Outremeuse.

Romantic CEMETERIES

147 PSYCHIATRIC HOSPITAL CEMETERY

Daalbroekstraat
Oud-Rekem
Limburg

No one ever visits this haunting cemetery deep in the woods on the edge of the Limburg national park. Overgrown and deserted, it is one of the saddest places in Belgium. It isn't even marked on local maps, so this is not the easiest place to find. You cannot enter the cemetery but it is possible to stand at the gate and see the rows of small crosses almost buried in the long grass. They mark the graves of psychiatric patients who were confined in a former castle in the nearby village of Oud-Rekem. Something like 1750 mainly male patients were buried in this remote spot between 1921 and 1981. Look closely and you will see rosary beads hanging from some of the crosses.
Located on a forest road opposite a modern hospital signed OPZC between cycle points 62 and 63.

148 MORTEHAN CHURCHYARD

Mortehan
Luxembourg

Mortehan is a sleepy village of grey slate houses located in a bend in the River Semois. Its old churchyard has survived in a grassy meadow where flowers grow wild and stray chickens peck around the gravestones. Most of the graves in this quiet spot date from the 17th and 18th centuries. The names of the people who once lived here have been eroded by the Ardennes rain, lost forever. But that just adds to the romance of this abandoned spot.

149 CAMPO SANTO

Visitatiestraat/
Verkortingstraat
Sint-Amandsberg
East Flanders

The overgrown Campo Santo cemetery clings to a hill in the Ghent suburb of Sint-Amandsberg. You might struggle to find the entrance, which is located at the far end. Founded in 1847, it contains the graves of famous Flemish writers, artists, poets and thinkers. Some are commemorated by massive stone monuments decorated with laurel wreaths, broken columns and weeping angels. Others have more unusual modern tombs. There is no map to guide you around, and no one seems to understand the layout, but it is interesting just to wander among the old tombs shaded by ancient trees. You might, if you are lucky, find the simple stone inscribed *Unter der Erde* (Below the Earth) where museum director Jan Hoet is buried, or the little metal table with a coffee cup and waffle marking the tomb of the comic book illustrator Marc Sleen.

150 DIEWEG

Dieweg 95
Uccle
Brussels

The old Brussels cemetery on the Dieweg is one of the most romantic spots in Brussels. Abandoned in 1958, its old stone tombs are covered in ivy and moss. Some people come here to wander among the dilapidated Gothic chapels, crumbling stone angels and sad faded photographs of the dead. But others are drawn by the rare species of moss and wild flowers in this untouched urban wilderness. Founded in 1866, the cemetery is dotted with mysterious tombs bearing Hebrew inscriptions from the time when this was one of the few cemeteries in Belgium to allow Jewish burials. But it takes some time to track down the tomb of Hergé, the Belgian illustrator who created Tintin. He was buried here in 1983, long after the cemetery had officially closed down.

151 LAEKEN CEMETERY

Parvis Notre-Dame
Laeken
Brussels

This old Brussels cemetery is filled with the grand tombs of eminent 19th-century Belgians. Former mayors and military leaders occupy prime spots on major avenues while artists and musicians are buried in the minor lanes. The Atelier Salu next to the entrance created many of the bronze figures of fainting girls and mourning women.

151 LAEKEN CEMETERY

SHIP LIFTS ON THE CANAL DU CENTRE

EXPERIENCES

Engineering WONDERS

152 **SHIP LIFTS ON THE CANAL DU CENTRE**
Rue Tout-Y-Faut 90
Houdeng-Goegnies
Hainaut
+32 (0)78 05 90 59
canalducentre.be

One of the great engineering projects of the 19th century is hidden away in the rust belt of Wallonia. The four ship lifts on the Canal du Centre were built in the 1880s to connect the Meuse and Scheldt rivers. Napoleon had already tried to build a canal to link northern France with the Ruhr region, but his engineers were defeated by a 70-metre ridge calling for 33 separate locks.
The problem was finally solved by building four hydraulic canal lifts. These astonishing wrought iron structures employ the laws of fluid mechanics to lift barges floating in huge watertight troughs.

152 SHIP LIFTS ON THE CANAL DU CENTRE

As the upper trough descends with a barge floating inside, the lower one is pushed up by water pressure. Designed by a British engineer, the lifts were opened by the Belgian king in 1888. They could raise a 300-tonne barge 17 metres in just a few minutes, using nothing more than water pressure. For more than a century, these lifts were a vital part of Europe's inland waterways, carrying barges laden with coal and gravel. They are now too small for huge modern barges, but have been preserved in working order by local enthusiasts, who run boat tours in the summer.
One of the old engine houses on the canal waterfront has been turned into a museum filled with scale models, plans and photographs. You can also look inside simple wooden huts where Italian mineworkers lived and visit a restored wooden barge. There is a cafe, but it is basic.
Boat trips are organised by Voies d'Eau du Hainaut.

153 PETIT LANAYE LOCKS

Petit Lanaye
Liège

The huge complex of three locks at Petit Lanaye was built in 1962 on the River Meuse to take barges sailing between Liège and Maastricht. An enormous fourth lock was added in 2016 to carry much larger modern barges. The locks stand next to the wide Albert Canal which passes through a canyon blasted out of the rock in the 1930s. The entire site has been landscaped as a visitor attraction with an observation deck overlooking the locks.

154 ANTWERP HARBOUR CRANES

154 ANTWERP HARBOUR CRANES

Rijnkaai,
near Hangar 27
Antwerp
havenkranen.be

Wander north along the Antwerp waterfront and you eventually reach a row of 17 abandoned harbour cranes. These giant machines were once used to unload cargo from ships in Antwerp harbour. They are now preserved by the MAS museum as examples of industrial technology. The oldest is a wooden crane from 1907. The more modern electric crane with the number 400 KA was built in 1950, while 410 KD dates from 1961.

155 TRAIN WORLD

GARE DE SCHAERBEEK
Place Princesse
Élisabeth 5
Schaerbeek
Brussels
+32 (0)2 224 74 69
trainworld.be

The spectacular train museum opened in 2016 in a renovated railway station in the Brussels suburb of Schaerbeek. The dramatic interior was conceived by Belgian comic strip artist François Schuiten, while the ominous background music was composed by Bruno Letort. You can climb on board a steam locomotive, peer inside a luxury sleeping car and inspect nostalgic railway officials' uniforms.

156 ZIMMER CLOCK

Zimmerplein 18
Lier
Antwerp
+32 (0)3 800 03 95
zimmertoren.be

The little town of Lier contains three extraordinary clocks constructed in the 1930s by the local watchmaker and amateur astronomer Louis Zimmer. He began by building a beautiful astronomical clock on the outside wall of an abandoned tower from the 14th century. It features two globes decorated in blue and gold and ten clock faces with signs of the zodiac, tides in Lier, phases of the moon, days of the month, months of the year and other arcane facts.

Zimmer went on to design a Wonder Clock which he exhibited at New York's World Fair in 1935. Described by the New York Museum of Science

as 'the outstanding wonder of the age', it is now displayed in a small pavilion next to the Zimmer Tower. Three years in the making, it was an extraordinary construction with 93 small dials and 14 automata. The various clocks display the time divisions of the world, the movements of the planets, high and low tides in the world's principal ports and dozens of other details. The fastest clock hands revolve once around the dial in one-hundredth of a second, while the slowest rotates once every 26.000 years.
A small crowd gathers each day on the square in front of the Zimmer Tower to watch a mechanical show on the side wall. An old man strikes a bell, the red shutters flip open and a series of portraits slowly slide into view, representing one hundred years of Belgian history.

156 ZIMMER CLOCK

Unusual STAIRS

157 **SIGNAL DE BOTRANGE**
Route de Botrange 133-B
Waimes
Liège

An inexplicable stone staircase leading nowhere stands behind the car park at the Signal de Botrange. It was built in 1923 on the highest spot in Belgium, in the middle of the bleak Hautes Fagnes moors. The land at this point is 694 metres above sea level, but the steps add a further six metres, bringing the height to a neat 700 metres. Eleven years later, a stone observation tower was built nearby, 18 metres above the ground, so the little stone staircase has no purpose any more.

158 **VLOOYBERGTOREN**
Oude Pastorie-straat 22
Tielt-Winge
Flemish Brabant

This strange unsupported iron staircase was built by the sculptor Yves Willems in 2013. Known as the Vlooybergtoren, it stands on a hill in a remote area of Flemish Brabant. You reach it on a narrow path that begins behind the former vicarage (now the local tourist office). The rusted metal structure rattles noisily as you climb the 57 steps. From the top, you get a spectacular view of lush cornfields and vineyards. Located near cycle point 27.

159 MONTAGNE DE BUEREN

Hors-Château
Liège

This incredibly steep staircase with 373 stone steps was built in Liège in 1881. *The Huffington Post* described it as 'the most extreme staircase in the world'. It leads from the old town straight up the steep hill leading to the citadel on the summit. Known as the Montagne de Bueren, it was originally built to allow soldiers to reach the garrison without having to use the old narrow alleys lined with bars and brothels. It takes its name from the 15th-century aristocrat Vincent de Bueren who saved the city from an attack by the Duke of Burgundy. The stairs link Féronstrée with Au Péri and the citadel.

159 MONTAGNE DE BUEREN

160 SINT-ROMBOUTS-TOREN

Onder den Toren 12
Mechelen
Antwerp
+32 (0)15 29 76 54
visit.mechelen.be/toren

You have to climb an ancient spiral staircase with 538 steps to reach the top of the St Rombouts tower in Mechelen. But it's worth the effort to reach the top of the 97-metre Gothic tower. When the weather is right, you can see all the way to the Atomium in Brussels and the port of Antwerp. A glass platform called the Skywalk was added in 2009 so you can now step out into the void for a sensational view.

161 MAS ROOFTOP

Hanzesteden-plaats 2
Antwerp
+32 (0)3 338 44 00
mas.be

A series of escalators in the MAS museum takes you up to the roof terrace on the tenth floor. As you rise through the building, the views become increasingly spectacular. Once you are out on the roof, you can see the old town, the massive port area and the Eilandje neighbourhood around the MAS. You don't pay to visit the terrace, which is normally open until late in the evening.

Unexpected VIEWS

162 PARK KEIZERSBERG

Leuven
Flemish Brabant

An old gate almost no one knows about leads up the hill to the Park Keizersberg in Leuven. Standing on the summit, you get a view of the old spires as well as the sprawling Stella Artois brewery. A castle once stood on this site, but nothing remains except a well and a ruined wall. The site is now occupied by a gloomy 19th-century Benedictine abbey. The grounds were turned into a public park in 2010. As you wander around, you may come across mysterious ruins, a hidden cemetery and an orchard with rare apple trees and a few sheep. Main entrance at Mechelsestraat 202, or climb the steps behind the OPEK cultural centre, off the Tramweg footpath.

163 VIEW OF ANTWERP FROM THE NOORDKASTEEL

Noordkasteel Zuid
Antwerp

It takes a little effort to find the view of Antwerp from the Noordkasteel. You need to head north, beyond the Red Star Line Museum, and cross the narrow bridge Royersbrug. A path to the left leads to a bend in the River Scheldt where you get a spectacular panoramic view of the city. It takes in the cathedral spire, Boerentoren, MAS museum and old harbour cranes. The site is called Noordkasteel after a 19th-century fort built here to defend the city, but nothing remains of the fort except a moat sometimes used as a swimming pool. Located between cycle points 54 and 55.

164 NAMUR FORTRESS

BEGIN THE CLIMB AT:
Rue du Grognon
Namur
+32 (0)81 24 73 70
citadelle.namur.be

You get some striking views of Namur from the citadel high above the town. But the best viewpoint is a spot most people walk past on their way to the top. You find it by taking the cobbled lane from the open space called Grognon next to the river. The route passes through a gate called Vieux Puits and climbs a series of broad steps designed for horses. Look for the square tower at the top, where you have a spectacular view of Namur's old houses and churches. Climb further up the hill and you reach a second viewpoint on a grassy plateau near a perfume workshop. You can also reach the citadel by a modern cable car that runs from a station next to the river at Place Maurice Servais. Launched in 2021, it replaces an older cable car that stopped running in 1997.

164 NAMUR FORTRESS

165 VIEW OF BRUSSELS FROM THABORBERG

Thaborstraat 11
Dilbeek
Flemish Brabant

The gently rolling Pajottenland countryside to the west of Brussels has barely changed since the 16th century when Pieter Bruegel the Elder visited local villages to paint works such as *The Blind Leading the Blind*. You can still find rural landscapes close to the city including the tiny nature reserve Thaborberg where you get an unexpected view of the Brussels skyline from a 77-metre summit. The reserve occupies the site of a country house built in 1903, but nothing remains except for a driveway and a ruined chapel wall buried in the trees.

166 LIÈGE BELVEDERE

PARC SAINT-LÉONARD
Rue Mathieu
Laensberg 32-50
Liège
visitezliege.be

It's a long climb up the hillside, but the view of Liège from the belvedere is spectacular. The trail is marked with small red arrows to keep you on the right route. It begins in the Parc Saint-Léonard, not far from the Grand Curtius museum, and climbs slowly up through the wood Bois des Carmelites. An iron staircase at the summit leads to a viewing platform high above the River Meuse with a sweeping view of the domes and spires of old Liège.

Unique NEIGHBOURHOODS

167 JEWISH QUARTER

**Hoveniersstraat
Antwerp**

A vibrant Jewish community lies hidden down the quiet back streets near Centraal Station in Antwerp. Here is one of the few places in Europe where Yiddish is still spoken. You see men dressed in Orthodox black costumes, busy kosher restaurants and small Sephardic synagogues. The Jews arrived in Antwerp in the late 19th century fleeing from pogroms in eastern Europe. Many had hoped to reach the United States on a Red Star Line steamer, but were stopped by illness or a lack of funds. They traded in diamonds, turning Antwerp into the world's diamond capital. Some 80 percent of the world's uncut diamonds are traded in one short street called Hoveniersstraat. Here you can still see Jewish dealers walking around with black briefcases filled with diamonds, securely chained to their belts. The Orthodox Jews in this tiny quarter preserve ancient traditions that have died out elsewhere in Europe. It is a place of strange contrasts, especially during the Purim festival when fathers in black suits accompany children dressed in gaudy Carnival costumes.

168 MATONGE QUARTER

Chaussée de Wavre and Rue de la Paix
Ixelles
Brussels

The Matonge lies on the edge of the European quarter, but nowhere in Belgium is less European. This neighbourhood was built in the late 19th century as an elegant bourgeois district, with a mix of neoclassical and art nouveau architecture. But it gradually evolved into an African neighbourhood in the 1960s, taking its name from a district in Kinshasa. The community developed around the Congolese student house Maison Africaine set up by a Belgian woman known affectionately as Mamma Monique. Now the neighbourhood is a cosmopolitan mix of African food stores, Belgian bars and Italian restaurants.

169 OUTREMEUSE

Rue Puits-en-Sock
Liège

Not many tourists cross the Pont des Arches in Liège to explore the left bank. They are missing the most authentic quarter of the city, where writers, artists and anarchists have settled for centuries. The crime writer Georges Simenon was born on the more respectable right bank, but spent most of his youth in Outremeuse, where he found inspiration for his Inspector Maigret novels. "Liège is present in all my novels, even if they are set in Nantes or Charleroi", he once wrote. This ancient quarter is still a fascinating warren of narrow lanes, religious shrines and strange processions, its fierce independence kept alive by the Commune Libre de Saint-Pholien-des-Prés.

170 **VOORHAVEN**

New-Yorkstraat
Ghent
East Flanders

It's rare for anyone to stumble on the old 19th-century harbour quarter in Ghent. This authentic maritime district to the north of the old town is a strange, undiscovered area with cobbled quays, massive cranes and abandoned railway tracks. The street names recall the time when ships sailed from here to London, Liverpool and even New York. Now the neighbourhood is slowly becoming fashionable as young people settle in restored industrial spaces.

170 VOORHAVEN

171 COGELS-OSYLEI

Cogels-Osylei
Antwerp

This grand avenue in an Antwerp suburb has some of the finest art nouveau and eclectic architecture in Belgium. The main street Cogels-Osylei is lined with buildings in every style imaginable, from mock-Greek temples to art nouveau. The exuberance continues in the surrounding streets where wealthy locals built grand houses decorated with turrets, balconies and ceramic tiles. This used to be a forgotten district with few restaurants, but the squares De Dageraadplaats, Tramplein and Draakplaats are now lively urban eating hubs.

172 DE HAAN CONCESSIE

Rembrandtlaan and surroundings
De Haan
West Flanders
visitdehaan.be

Most resorts along the Belgian coast are overwhelmed by modern apartments, but the little town of De Haan has kept its original charm. A favourite among royals, the seaside resort was laid out in the dunes in 1889 by the German urban planner Hermann-Josef Stübben. He insisted on winding lanes, quaint white villas in English country house style, and large gardens. The houses have romantic names like 'Little Red Riding Hood' and look like drawings in a German fairy story. Albert Einstein stayed for a few months in 1933 in the Villa Savoyarde before fleeing to the United States.

171 COGELS-OSYLEI

Authentic MARKETS

173 VRIJDAGMARKT
Vrijdagmarkt
Antwerp

Locals have been coming to the street auction on the Vrijdagmarkt in Antwerp since the 16th century. Here is where dealers sell off old office furniture from bankrupt firms, ornaments once cherished by someone's grandmother, and plastic bin bags filled with miscellaneous junk. The auction begins early on Friday morning around an ancient statue of St Catherine. The public stands behind a rope while an auctioneer wrapped in a heavy anorak shouts out prices. The man sitting in the tent next to a heater is the bailiff, who carefully notes the sales in a ledger. You might pick up a crystal vase worth ten times what you paid. Or you could go home with a sealed box filled with four old cardigans and a broken computer. Every Friday from 9 am to 1 pm.

174 BROCANTE DE SAINT-PHOLIEN
Boulevard de la Constitution
Liège

A lively flea market fills the neighbourhood around the Saint-Pholien church in Liège every Friday. It lies in the heart of the Outremeuse quarter where the writer Georges Simenon spent his youth. This is the perfect place to hunt for old Ella Fitzgerald records, ceramic ornaments and used Belgian army boots. You might even pick up a copy of Simenon's 1931 thriller *Le Pendu de Saint-Pholien* which is set in the neighbourhood. Every Friday from 6 am to 1 pm.

175 LES ÉCURIES VAN DE TRAM

Rue Rubens 95
Schaerbeek
Brussels
+32 (0)496 30 86 76

A weekly organic market is held in a restored industrial building in the Brussels commune of Schaerbeek. Originally used as stables for the horses that once pulled Brussels trams, the restored spaces are now occupied by small local producers on Fridays and Saturdays. You find unusual cheeses, a coffee bar and a food truck parked inside.

176 PRONDELMARKT

Sint-Jacobsmarkt
Ghent
East Flanders

A lively flea market is held in Ghent on a cobbled square behind the Sint-Jacobskerk on Friday, Saturday and Sunday mornings. The dealers set up stalls selling ancient electrical appliances, crates of vinyl records, dusty vases and the occasional stuffed zebra. The mood is lively, with people shouting in Ghent dialect, customers grabbing an early breakfast on a cafe terrace and the smell of fried potatoes wafting over from the chip stand. Every Friday from 9 am to 1 pm.

177 TONGEREN ANTIQUE MARKET

Leopoldwal,
Veemarkt, and
other locations
Tongeren
Limburg

The old Roman town of Tongeren hosts a lively antique market every Sunday. Established over 30 years ago, it brings together more than 300 dealers who spread out around the old town walls, along with 40 or so antique stores in town. It is the perfect place to haggle over the price of a rococo table or a vintage lamp to decorate an urban loft. Every Sunday from 6 am to 1 pm.

178 OSTEND VISTRAP

Visserskaai
Ostend
West Flanders

The quayside fish market in Ostend is a lively, friendly place where locals and tourists go to buy fresh sole and shrimps brought to shore just a few hours earlier. Many of the stands are run by fishermen's wives who remain cheerful even when a howling gale is blowing in from the North Sea.

178 OSTEND VISTRAP

179 BROCANTE DES BASTIONS

LES BASTIONS CAR PARK

Boulevard Walter de Marvis 22
Tournai
Hainaut

The historic town of Tournai is the setting for a lively flea market every Sunday morning. Held in an empty shopping centre car park, it's a friendly, popular event with an eclectic range of objects on sale. You might come across an old carved cupboard salvaged from an abandoned castle, or a rocking horse that has been gathering dust in someone's attic for six decades. It's fun to wander around the market even if you return home with nothing more than a set of six spoons.

Independent BREWERIES

180 **BRUSSELS BEER PROJECT**

Rue Antoine Dansaert 188
Brussels
beerproject.be

This fantastic brewing concept has brought fresh vitality to the Brussels craft beer scene. Launched as a crowdfunded initiative in 2013, the project has developed several fine beers including Delta and Grosse Bertha. The team went on in 2015 to open a little brewery in downtown Brussels where they host beer tastings and concerts.

181 **DE DOLLE BROUWERS**

Roeselare-straat 12-B
Diksmuide
West Flanders
oerbier.be

Here is a fantastic local brewery launched by three friends who call themselves 'De Dolle Brouwers', (The Mad Brewers). They took over a dilapidated brewery in the village of Esen near Diksmuide in 1980 and started brewing a limited range of six bottled beers. One of the Mad Brewers, Kris Herteleer, designs the quirky hand-drawn labels.

182 **OUD BEERSEL**

Laarheide-straat 230
Beersel
Flemish Brabant
+32 (0)2 680 79 54
oudbeersel.com

When the Oud Beersel brewery closed down in 2002, it looked like the end of the road for its distinctive Lambic beer. But two young enthusiasts have revived the brewery and reopened the old Bierhuis. They have won awards for their Oude Geuze Oud Beersel, including 'world's best Gueuze' and 'world's best sour beer' in 2016. Served in a chunky glass tumbler, this sour, complex beer has a rich flavour from cherries fermented in oak barrels.

183 BROUWERIJ KAZEMATTEN
Houten Paard 1
Ypres
West Flanders
+32 (0)57 38 80 21
kazematten.be

This brewhouse occupies ancient fortifications below the Ypres town walls. Launched in 2014 by the Sint-Bernardus brewery in Watou, it produces a golden ale called Grotten Santé and a light beer called Wipers Times (named after a World War One newspaper published here by British troops). You can drink the beers in a vast vaulted room below the city ramparts.

184 DE TROCH
Langestraat 20
Wambeek, Ternat
Flemish Brabant
+32 (0)2 582 10 27
detroch.be

This authentic 19th-century Lambic brewery is located in a brick farmhouse just outside Brussels. The friendly owners create Gueuze beers using ancient equipment. They sell bottles out in the courtyard or you can eat Flemish *stoverij* (stew) made with the brewery's prize-winning Chapeau beer in the relaxed local brasserie Leo's & Ben's.

180 BRUSSELS BEER PROJECT

Unique TRADITIONS

185 BEACH FLOWERS

Knokke, and other Belgian beach resorts
West Flanders

When Belgian kids spend summer at the beach, they like to set up little stands outside the family beach hut where they sell elaborate flowers made from coloured crepe paper attached to wooden rods. They have been doing this for more than a hundred years at all the resorts along the coast. The flowers are more complex and sophisticated than you would expect. They are bought by other children who pay with razor shells gathered on the beach. No one knows when it began, but this custom is unique to Belgium.

186 SHRIMP FISHERMEN

Oostduinkerke beach
West Flanders

You sometimes see shrimp fishermen riding huge workhorses through the streets of Oostduinkerke. It is one of the strangest sights on the coast. Dressed in bright yellow oilskins, they ride heavy Brabant draft horses through the sea dragging vast nets designed to catch small grey shrimps. The fishermen are now listed by UNESCO as part of the world's intangible cultural heritage.

187 DUCASSE

JARDIN DU MAYEUR
Grand'Place
Mons
Hainaut
+32 (0)65 33 55 80
museedudoudou.
mons.be

An ancient tradition in Mons involves young men fighting a bitter battle on the main square with a green dragon called Doudou. This strange ritual known as the Ducasse is held every year on the first Sunday after Pentecost. It features, among other things, participants dressed in green leaves, a swinging dragon's tail and a man representing St George who finally kills the creature with a single pistol shot. A Musée du Doudou opened in 2015 dedicated to this curious tradition.

188 MEYBOOM

Rue des Sables 39
Brussels
meyboom.be

Every year on August 9, locals dressed in uniforms gather in a dingy Brussels street near the Comic Book Museum to commemorate a battle fought back in 1213. During the ceremony, a team of strong men carry a large beech tree called the Meyboom from Grand-Place to the Rue des Sables, accompanied by musicians and a procession of giants. It is planted in the ground at around 5 pm to celebrate victory over an army from Ghent, or possibly Leuven. No one is quite sure of the story, but it is an excuse to drink a few glasses of beer on a summer evening.

THE RIVER LEIE

ADVENTURES

Baffling BORDERS

189 **NEUTRAL MORESNET**

GEULDALMUSEUM
Maxstrasse 9
Kelmis/
La Calamine
Liège
+32 (0)87 65 75 04
mvm-kelmis.be

This little Belgian town near the German border is one of the strangest places in Europe. For almost one hundred years, it was a neutral micro state with its own flag, tax system and language. You have to visit the local museum to discover the curious history of the town, now known as La Calamine in French, or Kelmis in German. In a series of dark, cluttered rooms, you discover that Moresnet was once a centre of zinc mining. The huge Vieille Montagne mine outside the town supplied zinc cladding for Paris rooftops. It also formed the basis of calamine lotion as well as providing the arms industry with a vital metal.

After the fall of Napoleon, when the map of Europe was being redrawn, the precious zinc mine lay between the Netherlands and Germany. In 1816, it was made a neutral territory called Neutral Moresnet marked out by 60 border stones.

The museum has some strange relics from the period when Moresnet had its own laws, a separate tax system and an independent currency. It even had its own postage stamps, although they could only be used within the town.

Neutral Moresnet was briefly the setting for one of the strangest utopian projects in history when the local doctor persuaded the micro state to change its name to Amikejo and adopt Esperanto as its official language. The state designed its own flag and created a national anthem. But the dream came to an abrupt end in 1914 when German troops occupied the town. Nothing now remains of the neutral country except for a few boundary stones dotted around the damp forest.

190 VENNBAHN ENCLAVE

Leykaul
Liège
vennbahn.eu

A narrow strip of Belgian territory was created after the First World War along the route of the Vennbahn railway line. Under the terms of the Treaty of Versailles, Germany gave Belgium this 28,5-kilometre corridor between Kalterherberg and Raeren. Under the agreement, Kalterherberg station was transferred to Belgium, but the village itself remained German. The treaty also created six German enclaves within Belgium including the village of Ruitzhof.

The abandoned railway line has now been turned into a Belgian cycling and walking trail, and almost all traces of the border have vanished. But you can still spot old border stones (marked P for Prussia on one side and B for Belgium on the other), abandoned road barriers and even the occasional Belgian flag deep within Germany. Almost no one is aware of this narrow Belgian corridor, although it is marked with astonishing accuracy on Google maps.

191 BAARLE-HERTOG

Baarle-Hertog
Antwerp

The town of Baarle-Hertog/Baarle-Nassau is one of the most confusing places in the world. It has two town halls, two post offices, two fire stations and even two legal systems, because it is partly Dutch and partly Belgian. It is hard to know where the border runs, as it is made up of 22 tiny Belgian enclaves located within the Netherlands, along with seven Dutch exclaves located within the Belgian enclaves. As a result, there are dozens of international frontier lines running through the town, each marked with a line of small white crosses. One frontier runs through a local cafe. Another border line passes straight through the middle of a front door, so the living room is in the Netherlands, but the kitchen lies in Belgium. The house has to have two doorbells and even two house numbers, as the address is Loveren 2 in Baarle-Hertog, but Loveren 19 over the border in Baarle-Nassau.

191 BAARLE-HERTOG

This complex situation originated in a series of mediaeval treaties in which land was transferred between the Lords of Breda and the Duke of Brabant. When the Dutch Republic split from the Spanish Netherlands in the 16th century, the plots of land where divided into Dutch (Nassau) and Spanish (Hertog). After Belgium split from the Netherlands in 1830, the border was finally settled by a commission after 15 years of discussing how to sort out the muddle.

One of the strangest sites is the Dodendraad, or death fence, which stands in a field outside the village. Built in 2008, it reconstructs a section of the 2000 volt electric fence put up by the German army in the First World War along the border between the Netherlands and Belgium. An electricity substation has also been rebuilt as a reminder of this vanished war zone.

192 THE MEUSE PENINSULA

Petit Lanaye
Liège

A narrow strip of land on the River Meuse became part of Belgium in the 1960s when the river changed direction. But the uninhabited peninsula could only be reached from the Dutch river bank, so it lay beyond the reach of the Belgian police. It became a popular spot for drug dealing and other illegal activities, but nothing was done until a corpse was discovered. The two countries began to negotiate a land exchange they finally settled in 2017. The Belgian peninsula became Dutch territory, while two smaller Dutch areas were given to Belgium. The new Belgian territory lies next to the Petit Lanaye locks, while the land given to the Dutch lies on the other side of the river.

Inspiring
TRAM AND METRO TRIPS

193 COAST TRAM
West Flanders
delijn.be

Most people tell you the same thing. The Belgian coast is ugly. It is just a long line of apartment buildings. The waiters are rude. The wind blows sand in your face. And so it goes on. But take a ride on the coast tram and you might see things differently. The 67-kilometre route is the longest tram ride in the world and costs just a few euro for a day ticket. You can cover the entire route from De Panne to Knokke in a couple of hours, but it is more fun to get off at different stops along the way. You can wander among the fish shops in Nieuwpoort, drink a coffee in Ostend's grand café Du Parc, and walk out to the end of the wooden jetty in Blankenberge. But the best part of the trip is the stretch along the sea just west of Ostend.

194 TRAM 44 TO TERVUREN
Brussels
stib.be

One of the most beautiful tram rides in the world, tram 44 starts in a gloomy underground station (Montgomery) but soon emerges on Avenue de Tervuren. It then rumbles past the stunning Stoclet House on the right and the tram museum on the left before plunging into the forest. The journey ends some 20 minutes later at a quaint 19th-century tram station in Tervuren.

195 TRAM 4 THROUGH GHENT

Ghent
East Flanders
delijn.be

It is not the fastest route, but tram 4 takes you on a gentle tour of Ghent, past the old city gate Rabot, the new law courts designed by Stéphane Beel and the old harbour quarter Sas van Gent where inland barges tie up for the night.

196 CHARLEROI METRO

Charleroi Sud station
Hainaut
infotec.be

One of the strangest ways to discover Charleroi is to take a ride on metro line M1 or M2. Starting at Charleroi Sud station, you take the metro in the direction of Anderlues. It passes through several underground stations, and eventually emerges on a dramatic elevated viaduct above a network of motorways, railway lines and canals. It is an astonishing experience, like a roller coaster ride above the city, taking you through a disturbing dystopian urban landscape of abandoned factories, cooling towers and spoil heaps. Leave at Providence station in Marchienne-au-Pont and wait for the next train back to Sud.

196 CHARLEROI METRO

Unknown URBAN TRAILS

197 LES COTEAUX DE LA CITADELLE

TRAILS BEGIN AT:
Impasse des Ursulines, off Montagne de Bueren
Liège
visitezliege.be

Most visitors to Liège never discover the orchards and meadows above the city. Once planted with vines, this steeply sloping landscape still has old fruit trees, grazing sheep and a few goats. But it's not too easy to find. You need to follow the marked trails around the citadel known as *les coteaux de la citadelle*. The easiest route to the top is the long flight of steps called Montagne de Bueren. But there is a more intriguing and less well-known route you can take. It begins in the Impasse des Ursulines, to the left of the Montagne. This leads to a beautiful cluster of old buildings in Maasland Renaissance style. Some belonged to a 17th-century Béguinage, while others were constructed in the 1960s.
You now climb up the slopes following a series of narrow lanes and stone steps. Sometimes you come to a dead end and have to try a different route. But eventually you will reach a gate leading into a wood known as the Bois des Mineurs. Here you are high above the old town looking down on the rooftops and spires.
Several other ways to reach the top are even harder to find. One route passes through the courtyard of an old town house behind the law courts at Rue du Palais 60. Another trail begins with a staircase built inside a modern house at Rue Pierreuse 38. You can find all five different trails marked on the Sentiers des Coteaux map available at the tourist office.

198 DIJLEPAD

Access from Onze-Lieve-Vrouwestraat (lanes next to numbers 115 and 143)
Mechelen
Antwerp
mechelen.be

A new wooden walkway along the River Dijle in Mechelen takes you past old waterfront houses, overgrown gardens and hidden squares. The walk is particularly romantic at night when the route is lit by thousands of tiny spotlights.
You can begin on the Zoutwerf, a former harbour with an impressive Renaissance house once owned by the guild of fishermen. Or you can dive into one of the narrow lanes running down to the water from Onze-Lieve-Vrouwestraat.
The trail follows a wooden walkway along a stretch of water once accessible only by boat. It ends at the Lamot cultural centre, where a bridge takes you across to the old fish market square. Near here is an old brown cafe called De Gouden Vis, which has a tiny hidden terrace at the back overlooking the water.

198 DIJLEPAD

199 BRUGES RAMPART WALK

Bruges
West Flanders
brugge.be

Millions of tourists head straight for the crowded centre of Bruges, but almost no one walks around the old ramparts. Landscaped in the 19th century, they form an almost continuous green belt around the old city. Here is where to head if you want to escape the crowds. You might pass the occasional fisherman or a local student on a bike, but almost no tourists come out this far. The seven-kilometre trail takes you past city gates, forgotten windmills and a wooden crane, with authentic local cafes like De Windmolen providing stops along the way.

200 GHENT NIGHT WALK

Sint-Michielsbrug
Ghent
East Flanders
visit.gent.be

Ghent is an atmospheric city after dark thanks in part to an inspiring new urban light plan launched in 1998. The ancient Gothic buildings like the Vleeshuis and the Gravensteen are now illuminated with subtle lights to highlight the mediaeval details, while spotlights in the pavements cast theatrical shadows on the walls. Begin a night walk on Sint-Michielsbrug and follow the waterfront north to the Vrijdagmarkt. Then head east to the streets around the Sint-Jacobskerk to find a friendly bar.

201 SINT-ANNA TUNNEL

Sint-Jansvliet
Antwerp

Many people don't realise you can walk under the River Scheldt in Antwerp. Just over half a kilometre long, the white tiled Sint-Anna tunnel was built in 1933. You find the entrance in an art deco brick building behind the basketball court on Sint-Jansvliet. A creaky wooden escalator takes you down to the tunnel level where you can walk to the other side in about ten minutes. But what do you do once you have made the crossing? In the past, people headed along the waterfront to the Sint-Anna beach, a strange resort once fashionable in the 1930s. Locals still come here to eat in the fish restaurants, swim in an open-air pool and cycle along the dike towards the Dutch border. But it isn't really a beach resort anymore.

Unusual BOAT TRIPS

202 LIÈGE RIVER BOATS

Quai de la Goffe 13
Liège
+32 (0)4 221 92 91
navettefluviale.be

It's now possible to see Liège from the river by taking a new river shuttle called La Navette Fluviale. It runs every hour, with six stops along the river including La Boverie, the Grand Curtius museum and the historic centre. Sit on the upper deck for a surprising view of this ancient and overlooked city or shelter down below when it rains. Tickets cost one euro for each stop. River boats run every day from April to October.

203 WAULSORT FERRY

Waulsort
Namur

Waulsort used to be a stylish resort on the River Meuse with a train station, elegant hotels and several restaurants. It is now a forgotten village near the French border where almost no one visits. But there is still a ferryman to take you across the river in the summer. Dating from 1871, the wooden barge is slowly pulled by hand using a submerged cable. The free service runs from April to September.

204 ROGER RAVEEL FERRY

Visserskaai
Ostend
West Flanders

Look out for the free ferry departing from the Aquarium in Ostend to the old docks on the other side of the harbour. The little ferry carries foot passengers and cyclists to a relatively quiet area on the east side of the harbour, where trails lead to an old Napoleonic fort and a quiet beach just behind the dunes. The ferry is named after the Belgian artist Roger Raveel, who decorated the side of the boat.

205 BERLARE

Berlare
East Flanders

A little yellow ferry takes cyclists and hikers across the River Dender every half hour. It forms a useful link in a network of quiet cycle routes along towpaths on either side of the river. Overlooking the landing stage on the north bank, the local bar 't Veerhuis is popular with local cycle teams stopping off for a Belgian beer. Located between cycle points 76 and 77.

204 ROGER RAVEEL FERRY

Cool BIKE RIDES

206 VENNBAHN CYCLE TRAIL

Sankt Vith
Liège
vennbahn.eu

The Vennbahn railway used to run through the wild Hautes Fagnes region of Belgium carrying raw materials to Germany. It closed down in 2008, leaving behind abandoned tracks and empty stations. But an ambitious project was launched in 2013 to turn it into a cycling and walking trail. The route now runs for 125 kilometres between Troisvierges in northern Luxembourg and Aachen in Germany. It takes you through deep pine woods and desolate stretches of the Fagnes. One of the best sections runs from the abandoned station Sourbrodt Gare to the pretty valley town of Monschau in Germany. Stop here for lunch before returning by the Rur Bank cycle route.

207 THE RIVER LEIE

Ghent
East Flanders
fietsnet.be

You can rent a bike in Ghent and set off down the River Leie on quiet cycle paths that avoid the busy roads. After twenty minutes of gentle cycling, you come to a complex series of bridges that takes you under a railway line and over a canal. Then you are out in the countryside cycling through quiet villages and watery meadows. The route sometimes follows the River Leie, meandering through the landscape like the Thames in England or the Vecht in the Netherlands. There are cafes along the way where you can sit by the water watching the boats go past. Follow cycle numbers 4, 52, 55, 56, 62, 57, 68, 52.

208 CYCLE THROUGH WATER

Bokrijk, Genk
Limburg
fietsnet.be

A cycle trail near Bokrijk open air museum includes a stretch called Cycle through Water. It takes you on a metal bridge sunk below a pond so you are literally under the water. The short stretch through water provides an unusual view of ducks floating past at eye level.
The route is signed from the Bokrijk car park as 'Fietsen door het water' (Cycle through Water). It forms part of a plan to attract cyclists to Limburg by creating exciting new experiences, such as cycling across the moors and cycling through the Kanne caves. Located between cycle points 243 and 91.

209 OSTEND HINTERLAND

Ostend
West Flanders
visitoostende.be

Most people struggle to find a parking place at the coast, but Ostend has come up with a smart solution. You can park on the edge of town and then hop on a free bike to get around. Launched back in 1998, the Park & Bike scheme lets visitors pick up distinctive bright yellow bikes at three locations. You can be at the beach in a few minutes, or, if you want to be more adventurous, set off on the 30-km Groen Lint route around the edge of Ostend, taking in a race course, oyster farm, fishermen's church and free ferry. Download the route map from the tourist office website.

210 LEUVEN HILL COUNTRY

Leuven
Flemish Brabant
fietsnet.be

The university town of Leuven sits in a valley with low hills to the east. You can take a bike to roam around this peaceful countryside dotted with old abbeys, farmhouses and even vineyards. But you might meet some surprisingly steep hills along the way like the horrendous sunken road Holleweg. The route takes you past Arenberg university campus, Park Abbey, Kessel-Lo park and the authentic country inn In Den Rozenkrans. Follow cycle numbers: 11, 84, 25, 83, 5, 80, 33, 11.

211 CYCLE IN THE TREES

THE PIJNVEN
Kiefhoekstraat 16
Hechtel-Eksel
Limburg
bosland.be/ontdek-bosland/fietsen/3

Deep in the pine woods of Bosland nature reserve, cyclists can ride up a gently sloping circular ramp to reach the tree tops, ten metres above the ground. Opened in 2019, *Fietsen door de bomen* is the latest project to bring cyclists to the wild forested landscape of Limburg. Architects De Gregorio & Partners have created a stunning structure supported on rugged rust-red steel stilts that merge seamlessly with the lofty pine trunks. Once you have circled the trees, you can set off through the Bosland woods on a series of numbered routes, and end up in the bike-friendly cafe De Lage Kempen.

Adventures with **KIDS**

212 BAREFOOT WALKING TRAIL

Stalkerweg
Zutendaal
Limburg
+32 (0)89 25 50 60
lieteberg.be

Kids can take off their shoes and socks to set off on a barefoot ramble through a reclaimed landscape near the Dutch town of Maastricht. Created in 2006 at De Lieteberg nature reserve, the two-kilometre 'Blotevoetenwandeling' trail (Barefoot Walking trail) leads across different types of terrain including grass, wood chippings, mud and shallow water. The route includes a steep hill, a stretch of water and a wooden lookout tower. Children, not surprisingly, love this experience. Lockers are provided for shoes.

213 BOEKENBERG SWIMMING POOL

Van Baurscheit-laan 88
Deurne
Antwerp
+32 (0)3 411 19 95
antwerpen.be

The open-air pool in Boekenberg Park was converted in 2007 into the country's first eco swimming pool. The German landscape architect firm Dongus lined the pool floor with more than 22.000 aquatic plants to maintain the water purity. It is now one of the best pools for a summer swim, but it can get crowded on hot days.

214 SEAFRONT

Vismijnstraat 7
Zeebrugge
West Flanders
+32 (0)50 55 14 15
seafront.be

The abandoned fish auction sheds in Zeebrugge harbour have been gradually converted to create the vibrant Seafront maritime park. The latest transformation ended in early 2022 when the complex reopened with a new range of activities and exhibitions linked to the North Sea. The waterfront site also has several pop-up shops, along with bright food trucks parked along the restored cobbled quays in the summer.

215 DE LUSTIGE VELODROOM

Blankenberge beach
West Flanders
+32 (0)496 25 72 54
delustigevelodroom.be

Belgian kids love to lark around on wonky bicycles at the ancient wooden velodrome on Blankenberge beach. Dating back to 1933, it rents out eccentric bicycles that are almost impossible to ride along the bumpy wooden cycle track. Some kids join in the fun, while others like to stand at the side watching the madness.

216 PARC JOSAPHAT MINI GOLF

Avenue Ambassadeur Van Vollenhoven
Schaerbeek
Brussels
+32 (0)486 23 70 69

The most beautiful mini golf in Belgium is squeezed onto a narrow strip next to the Parc Josaphat in Brussels. The course was designed by Belgian landscape architect René Pechère while working on grand designs elsewhere in the country. Pechère approached the task with his usual intellectual rigour and visited mini golf courses around Belgium before developing his design. The end result is a beautiful landscaped course next to a little cafe. Open Wednesdays and weekends.

214 **SEAFRONT**

LOMMELSE SAHARA

LANDSCAPES

Lost LANDSCAPES

217 LOMMELSE SAHARA

Lommel
Limburg
toerismelommel.be

The Lommelse Sahara is a strange desert landscape of pure white sand planted with pine trees. It occupies an abandoned industrial site in the Kempen region where quartz sand was once mined and a polluting zinc factory killed off all the trees. This bleak wilderness was later used by a weapons manufacturer to test grenades, but it has been turned into a nature reserve, with hiking trails, an observation tower and a lake in the former quarry.

218 DOODE BEMDE

START AT:
Neerijse
Flemish Brabant

The landscape of the Doode Bemde is quite different from anywhere else in Belgium. The River Dijle meanders sluggishly between waterlogged fields where little grows except poplars and reeds. Beyond a railway line, you can follow two marked trails (blue or red) through this ancient desolate landscape. A short detour off the blue route brings you to a secluded bird hide on the edge of a small lake.

You may be wondering if there is anywhere for lunch. Look out for the large church with two Romanesque towers on a hill to the south of the nature reserve. It stands in the village of Neerijse, where the village brewery De Kroon has been revived by a professor from Leuven University. It's the perfect spot to stop for some Belgian food and a De Kroon beer.

219 HET ZWIN

Graaf Léon
Lippensdreef 8
Knokke-Heist
West Flanders
+32 (0)50 60 70 86
zwin.be

A silent area of watery salt marshes and windswept dunes lies close to the beach town of Knokke. This was once the broad estuary of the Zwin, where 15th-century merchant ships carried English wool and Italian silk to Bruges. But the river silted up in the 16th century, turning Bruges into a dead port. The estuary slowly evolved into a desolate and watery landscape enclosed by dunes and pine woods. More than 100 different species of birds gather in this habitat, including Kentish plovers, crested larks and avocets. Several marked trails lead across this strange landscape on the border with the Netherlands.

219 HET ZWIN

220 HOGE KEMPEN NATIONAL PARK

Zetellaan 54
Eisden,
Maasmechelen
Limburg
+32 (0)89 65 56 65
nationaalpark hogekempen.be

This national park was created a few years ago in an area of abandoned mines close to the Dutch border. It's an inspiring conservation project copied by other countries. The park has four main entry points leading to vast areas of woodland and heath with the odd mining relic poking up out of the ground.
The main entrance to the park stands close to a coal mine abandoned in 1987. Here you find a visitors centre, a large cafe and a playground. You pay a small fee here to walk along marked trails and climb to the top of an abandoned slag heap for a sweeping view of woodland and flooded quarries.

Secret GARDENS

221 BAGGAERTSHOF

Sint-Jansstraat 37
Kortrijk
West Flanders
kortrijk.be/adressen/baggaertshof

This modest almshouse is hidden in the centre of Kortrijk near the K shopping centre. It isn't always open, so seize the chance if the little door is unlocked. You enter a quiet complex of 13 small whitewashed almshouses built in 1638 for 'unmarried women of unblemished character'. The beautiful overgrown apothecary garden is planted with mediaeval medicinal herbs and a lovely mulberry tree. The tiny almshouses around the garden have been turned into a children's play village.

222 JAPANSE TUIN

Gouv. Verwilghen-singel 23
Hasselt
Limburg
+32 (0)11 23 96 66
japansetuin.be

The Japanese garden in Hasselt is the largest in Europe, but it's still quite small. It is squeezed into a little site on the edge of town next to the ring road. You might have trouble finding it, but that doesn't mean you shouldn't visit, especially in blossom time. It was created in the early 1990s by a team of skilled Japanese gardeners who landscaped the modest site with a flowing river, small hill, waterfall, tea house and even a pebbly beach. The cherry blossom is gorgeous in the spring, but it is a beautiful peaceful spot at other times of the year. It's a pity there is nowhere for lunch, but you can head into Hasselt to eat at the stunning brasserie Het Smaaksalon (*smaaksalon.be*), which is located in a mansion decorated with pillars, chandeliers and oil portraits.

223 COLOMA ROSE GARDEN

Joseph Depauwstraat 25
Sint-Pieters-Leeuw
Flemish Brabant
natuurenbos.be/coloma

Located in the grounds of Coloma castle, this is one of the largest rose gardens in Europe. More than 66.000 roses have been planted here, including ancient species and rare varieties from all over the world. The garden is divided into countries, so you can study typical British roses or wander among tough species that survive in Canada. This is an enchanting spot in the summer months, with secret corners, hidden benches and odd windows cut in box hedges to provide unexpected views. Open Tuesday to Sunday.

224 THE GARDENS OF RUE NAIMETTE

Rue Naimette
Liège

The steep cobbled lane Rue Naimette in Liège is known as Little Montmartre. It's perhaps a slight exaggeration, but this is a lovely spot near the city centre with secret gardens hidden behind high stone walls. The gardens are private, but you can hear birdsong, smell the lilac blossom and occasionally glimpse inside a romantic urban retreat. At the top of the hill, take the Grande Randonnée hiking trail back into the old town. Simply follow the red and white markers.

225 HANGING GARDENS OF THUIN

Grand'Rue
Thuin
Hainaut
thuin.be

It hardly seems possible, but the little town of Thuin, not far from Charleroi, has ancient hanging gardens built on the steep hillside overlooking the River Sambre. Reached by cobbled lanes, the gardens were recently restored to create a fascinating trail running past small allotments, old city gates and an unexpected vineyard where they produce a few hundred bottles of Clos des Zouaves red wine every year.

226 LES JARDINS D'ANNEVOIE

Rue des Jardins d'Annevoie 37-A
Annevoie-Rouillon
Namur
+32 (0)82 67 97 97
annevoie.be

Deep in the woods in a remote corner of the Ardennes, the gardens at Annevoie are almost forgotten. You might be the only visitor on a quiet morning, yet these are among the most elaborate water gardens in Europe. They were created in the 18th century by Charles-Alexis de Montpellier, who borrowed ideas from landscaped gardens he had seen during his travels in Italy, France and England. Begun in 1758, the garden incorporates more than 50 water features including fountains, waterfalls and a grand canal. The former coach house has been converted into a restaurant with a terrace overlooking the gardens. The menu offers innovative dishes featuring locally caught trout, Ardennes sausages and Sommière cheese, along with craft beers and wines from the nearby Bioul estate.

227 THE GARDEN OF SMELLS

CHÂTEAU DE NAMUR
Rue de l'Ermitage 1
Namur

The Belgian garden historian Catherine Mathys has created an intriguing collection of six small gardens in the grounds of the Château de Namur. Located on the citadel hill above Namur, the gardens have 350 plant varieties grouped according to different properties. You will find a garden of emotions, a lavender garden and a taste garden, but perhaps the most curious is the garden of strange smells, which is devoted to plants that give off particularly unpleasant odours. Always open, free.

228 GODSHUIS SINT-JOZEF

Nieuwe Gentweg 24-32
Bruges
West Flanders

Look out for the open door on the Nieuwe Gentweg in Bruges. It leads into an unexpected garden where crocuses push through the soil in early spring. One of 44 almshouses dotted around the city, Godshuis Sint-Jozef was built in the 17th century as a home for the poor. Hidden from the street by high white-washed walls, the gardens are planted with ancient trees, rose beds and low box hedges.

229 PLANTIN-MORETUS GARDEN

Vrijdagmarkt 22
Antwerp
+32 (0)3 221 14 50
museumplantin moretus.be

Here is a beautiful baroque garden hidden within the walls of the Plantin-Moretus Museum in Antwerp. Created in 1639 by the printer Balthasar Moretus, it is modelled on an Italian formal garden. A small garden was added behind the museum shop in 2002. Designed by the Belgian landscape gardening firm Wirtz International, it is a simple design with brick paving, clipped trees and an undulating hedge.

228 GODSHUIS SINT-JOZEF

Romantic **PARKS**

230 HOF TER SAKSEN

Haasdonkbaan 101
Beveren
East Flanders
+32 (0)473 27 60 85
hortus-ter-saksen.be

The curious 19th-century Hof ter Saksen is surrounded by beautiful rambling grounds planted with ancient trees. The house was occupied by the German military in the First World War, and remained a ruin until just a few years ago. It has now been carefully restored, along with the former stables and orangery. You can wander in the herb garden, get lost in the arboretum or follow a meandering boardwalk through a small nature reserve. There is also a cobbled road leading to an orchard with grazing sheep and more than seventy varieties of fruit trees, while the former orangery has been turned into a summer cafe serving local beers.

231 SINT-PIETERSABDIJ

Sint-Pietersplein 12
Ghent
East Flanders
sintpieters abdijgent.be

A secret park lies hidden behind the Sint-Pieters-abdij (St Peter's Abbey) in Ghent. Entered by an old coach gate, this romantic spot dates back to the 9th century when the sloping land above the River Scheldt was terraced to create a vineyard. The site was restored in 1983 and replanted with fruit trees, vines and rare quinces. It is popular with students, but you sometimes have the place all to yourself.

232 KONINGSPARK

Koninginnelaan
Ostend
West Flanders

Almost no one notices the little gate opposite an abandoned swimming pool in Ostend. It leads into a walled garden created for King Leopold II in 1903 by the French landscape architect Elie Lainé. It is now an overgrown site with stone vases and four cast iron statues copied from originals in the gardens of Versailles. But there is a further mystery hidden behind a white wall in the middle of the garden. Here you find a tiny Japanese garden laid out in 2001 on the site of a pool. But it is only open at weekends in summer.

233 JANSENIUSPARK

Pater Damiaanplein
Leuven
Flemish Brabant

This little park next to the River Dijle in Leuven opened in 2017 on the site of a car park. From here you can see two ancient round towers on the banks of the Dijle that have been hidden for centuries. Originally built in the 12th century as part of the city defences, they were abandoned when Leuven expanded around 1360. One tower became known as the Janseniustoren after the Dutch theologian Jansenius, who renovated it in 1618 and lived there for eight years. Enter the gate on Pater Damiaanplein, next to the Holland College. The park is reached across a bridge at the end of the lane.

234 PARC DE LA BOVERIE

Rue du Parc
Liège

One of the most romantic parks in the country was created in the 19th century on a long island in the River Meuse. Located near Liège-Guillemins station, the Parc de la Boverie has winding footpaths, little stone bridges and symbolic sculptures. You can walk through the park to the tip of the island and sit on a bench watching huge river barges sail past. It's a peaceful spot that feels a little like Paris.

234 PARC DE LA BOVERIE

Dark **FORESTS**

235 BOIS JACQUES

Located on the road from Foy to Bizory
Luxembourg

The Bois Jacques lies on a quiet road running between the villages of Bizory and Foy. Deep within this dense pine forest near Bastogne, you come across some unexpected relics of war. The ground is pitted with holes dug by American soldiers during the winter battle of 1944-45. They fought here in freezing temperatures to liberate the tiny village of Foy at the bottom of the hill.
A small monument was put up next to the road in 2015, close to the hidden foxholes, but it has been attacked by vandals. An unmarked path to the left of the monument leads to a cluster of handmade wooden crosses planted in the forest to commemorate the soldiers of Easy Company, whose story inspired the TV series *Band of Brothers*. It's a quiet, haunting spot where visitors sometimes plant little American flags beside the foxholes.

236 FORÊT DE SOIGNES

South of Brussels
zonienwoud.be

The vast primeval beech forest to the south of Brussels has remote areas where the landscape has barely changed since the Ice Age. You discover deep valleys carved out by glaciers and forested areas untouched for hundreds of years. Three areas of the forest have been listed as UNESCO World Heritage because of their scientific interest. But it takes time to find these abandoned areas of woodland where fallen trees are left to decay and rare wild mushrooms flourish. The largest tract is the Joseph Zwaenepoel reserve, deep in the forest near Groenendaal station. To reach the Forêt de Soignes, take tram 8 to Coccinelles, or metro to Herrmann-Debroux.

237 KLANKENBOS SOUND FOREST

DOMMELHOF PARK
Toekomstlaan 5
Neerpelt
Limburg
+32 (0)11 61 05 10
klankenbos.be

You find more than 15 experimental sound installations by international artists dotted around the Klankenbos woods. The works include a vibrating stack of wooden boxes, an enormous flute you can walk inside and a glass box entered by an underground passage where you experience pure silence.

238 ZOET WATER

Maurits Noëstraat
Oud-Heverlee
Flemish Brabant
+32 (0)16 26 76 20
(Flemish Brabant tourist office number)

The forest trails at Zoet Water are popular on a Sunday, but they are often deserted on other days. Beginning at the Zoet Water ponds, you can follow old tracks and sunken lanes through the woods. They lead into a varied landscape of ancient forest and neat farms. At the end of a walk, you can sit with a beer in one of the local cafes overlooking the lake.

239 MUZIEKBOS

START AT:
La Salettestraat
Ronse
East Flanders
natuurenbos.be/muziekbos

The Hallerbos was once a secret beech wood where locals went to look at the bluebells in late April and early May. But these ancient woods near Brussels are now mobbed with visitors, so you now need to travel a little further from Brussels. You might try the Muziekbos (Music Woods) near Ronse, where you can wander along marked trails through bluebell woods on the language border between Wallonia and Flanders.

239 MUZIEKB

Adventurous **HIKES**

240 VALLÉE DE LA HOËGNE

Roquez 49
Sart
Liège
tourisme jalhaysart.be

The steep climb up the narrow Valley of the Hoëgne is one of the most attractive hikes in the Ardennes. The trail begins in a car park reached by driving across a ford in the river at Jalhay-Sart. The starting point is marked by a rustic wooden arch put up in 1899 when Queen Marie-Henriette opened the walk to the public. The trail follows the river upstream across several narrow bridges and wooden walkways. There are shady spots where children can play in the water and modest waterfalls named after Leopold II and his wife Marie-Henriette.

The woods become wilder and more deserted as you climb up the valley until all you can hear is the sound of the river splashing on the mossy rocks. It takes about 90 minutes to reach the rustic bridge known as the Passerelle du Centenaire at the upper end of the valley. You can continue to the village of Hockai, where there are several cafes and restaurants, and return along the abandoned railway line that once ran between Stavelot and Sart-Station.

241 LA BOUCLE NOIRE IN CHARLEROI

Charleroi
Hainaut
cheminsdesterrils.be

It's maybe not for everyone, but fearless walkers can follow a 20-kilometre trail through the industrial wasteland around Charleroi. Created by two indie rock musicians, this unexpected ramble incorporates canal towpaths, disused railway lines and an abandoned tunnel. Beginning at Charleroi Sud station, you wander through an unreal landscape of overhead roads, rusting factories and abandoned spoil heaps. But the Boucle Noire walk also takes in historic castles, street art and a bird sanctuary. The two musicians have even put together a list of tracks by local bands to play along the route. And if 20 kilometres seems a bit too ambitious, you can just do the four-kilometre industrial stretch between Charleroi Sud and Marchienne-au-Pont, then take the metro back into town. The Chemins des Terrils (Slag Heaps Trail) website has a detailed map and route description.

241 LA BOUCLE NOIRE

242 **GR 573**

SIGNAL DE BOTRANGE
Rue de Botrange 133
Robertville
Liège

The long-distance hiking trail GR 573 crosses the bleak upland region known as the Hautes Fagnes where nothing much can survive apart from tough heather and a few isolated pine trees. The route passes the Signal de Botrange, a wooden watchtower built in 1933 on the highest spot in Belgium, just short of 700 metres.
No one lives in this cold, marshy region of Europe. You sometimes have to walk along raised wooden bridges to avoid the eerie marshes, and at one point pass a cross where two lovers died in a snowstorm. The only building is an ancient inn where travellers have been sheltering from the wind and rain for centuries. Even in summer, the mist can come down suddenly, wrapping everything in a sinister silence.

243 **SINT-PIETERSBERG**

START AT:
Statieplein
Kanne
Limburg
toerismelimburg.be

The Sint-Pietersberg hill is one of the strangest border regions in Europe. Rising between the River Maas and the Albert Canal, this hill of soft marl stone has been quarried over the centuries to create a hidden network of caves. The frontier between the Netherlands and Belgium is marked out here by iron border posts dating from 1843. But there is a second invisible border separating French-speaking Belgium from Dutch-speaking Belgium. You can follow several marked trails through this unique limestone landscape starting in the village of Kanne. One route, marked with orange crosses, leads you past a Dutch vineyard, an abandoned Cold War bunker and a huge lock complex.

244 NISRAMONT

BARRAGE
DE NISRAMONT
Rue du Barrage
Nisramont
Luxembourg

One of the best wild hikes in the Ardennes takes you around a vast lake formed by the Nisramont Dam. The trail begins at the concrete dam built across the River Ourthe in the 1950s. After a steep climb, the path follows the meandering course of the river, with steep rocky sections and even staircases along the way.
The route leads to a spot where two branches of the Ourthe come together. Then you hike on, cross two footbridges and finally reach the opposite bank of the river. But you still have to hike a couple of hours before you are back at the dam. The circuit is marked as 13 kilometres, but everyone agrees it feels more like 18 kilometres. You should allow about five hours to do the entire route.

245 BAYEHON WATERFALL TRAIL

MOULIN DE BAYEHON
Rte du Bayehon 64
Malmedy
Liège

A hiking trail runs up from the Moulin de Bayehon to the second highest waterfall in Belgium. It's a romantic spot for a picnic, although the waterfall itself is not particularly spectacular. From here, follow the rust-brown stream further up the wooded valley, past a historic oak tree, until the path emerges on the boggy Hautes Fagnes. This is a strangely deserted spot where you can sometimes spot deer in the distance. The trail back to the Moulin runs through the dramatic canyon of the Pouhon stream.

246 FONDRY DES CHIENS

Nismes (Viroinval)
Namur

A trail runs from the village of Nismes to a spectacular limestone gorge deep in the Ardennes. This jagged landscape was formed millions of years ago as rain water slowly dissolved the soft chalk rock. Excavations have discovered ancient tools and human remains dating back 20.000 years. It seems likely neolithic tribes threw their dead into the deep fissures. They became known as *fondrys* in Roman times because they provided iron for local foundries. The *Fondry des Chiens* apparently gained its name because locals threw their dead dogs down the pit. The tourist office has marked out a four-kilometre trail from the village church to the gorge. But there is a longer hike across a chalk upland where rare flowers grow in the spring.

247 CRÊTES DE FRAHAN

Route de Alle
Rochehaut
Luxembourg

Several adventurous hikes begin at a viewpoint on the River Semois near the village of Rochehaut. The starting point is high above a bend in the river looking down on the village of Frahan. A steep path leads down to the river, where a footbridge built in 1924 takes you across to Frahan. The rustic cafe La Passerelle next to the bridge is a friendly spot to stop for coffee and homemade cake.
The walk number 1 from Frahan climbs the steep wooden hill behind the church to reach a ridge high above the river. Here you see several strange rock formations along with scattered remains of a 13th-century castle. The trail returns to Frahan along the river, but there are other paths you can follow to reach more remote spots. The Hôtel Beau Séjour is a friendly traditional hotel in Frahan with a typical Ardennes restaurant.

AFRO
Stork

SHOPPING

Unique SHOP INTERIORS

248 HAIRDRESSERS OF THE MATONGE

Chaussée de Wavre
and nearby streets
[Matonge district]
Ixelles
Brussels

The Matonge district in Brussels has a strong African spirit that dates back to the early 1960s. The neighbourhood is dotted with African hairdressers serving as informal community centres. They remain open until late at night as women sit getting their hair done, business deals are discussed, children do their homework and parcels are collected.

249 CHARCUTERIE DEPUYDT

Neermarkt 2
Ypres
West Flanders
+32 (0)57 20 05 33
charcuterie depuydt.be

The Depuydt family's butcher shop in Ypres was destroyed during the First World War, but rebuilt in 1922 using the old plans. So the interior looks much as it did in 1908 when the shop first opened. This is the only place in Ypres where you can buy pâté made with Sint-Bernardus Abt 12 beer. This shop also sells a delicious Ypres pâté made with Calvados as well as an old-style *boerenpâté* based on a 1907 recipe.

250 ROMBAUX

Mallebergplaats 13
Bruges
West Flanders
+32 (0)50 33 25 75
rombaux.be

This beautiful family business located in an old Bruges town house is a reminder of the days before the internet killed off the music store. It is worth going inside just to wander through the labyrinth of small rooms with their original mosaic floors, stained glass and wood panelling. Run by the same family for three generations, Rombaux is crammed with every imaginable genre from rare classical composers to new Flemish folk. Shopping here is so much richer than clicking on the internet.

251 FREDERIEK VAN PAMEL

Ezelstraat 33
Bruges
West Flanders
+32 (0)50 34 44 80
frederiek vanpamel.be

The Bruges florist Frederiek van Pamel has built up a reputation for creating stunning floral arrangements for special events. He moved in late 2017 to a large town house in the cobbled Ezelstraat where he sells stylish house plants, gardening tools and exotic floral bouquets.

252 ANIMAUX SPÉCIAUX

Mechelsestraat 17 (shop) and 73 (atelier)
Leuven
Flemish Brabant
+32 (0)497 66 17 64
animauxspeciaux.be

Taxidermist Jeroen Lemaitre works in a cluttered atelier in Leuven where he creates eccentric taxidermy art. His wondrous little shop in the same street is filled with exotic butterflies in bell jars, extraordinary framed insects, animal skulls and vintage posters printed with insects.

253 GANTERIE A. BOON

Lombardenvest 2
Antwerp
+32 (0)3 232 33 87
glovesboon.be

This little shop has been selling gloves since 1928 in a handsome interior lined with tiny wooden drawers. It still has the original tiled floor, wooden counter and an ancient cash register painted to look like wood. The shop stocks a range of styles from simple black leather gloves to stylish zebra print.

254 APOTHEEK DRYEPONDT

Wollestraat 7
Bruges
West Flanders

This pharmacy (*apotheek*) has stood on a narrow street facing the cloth hall in Bruges since 1835. The interior lined with beautiful old shelves dates from 1901. It was once famous for its nerve powders, but now mainly serves tourists who have developed a stomach bug or migraine.

255 APOTHEEK MUYLAERT

Brederodestraat 63
Antwerp

This beautiful Antwerp pharmacy has been handing out medicines since it opened 1902. The authentic Flemish Renaissance interior incorporates a wooden counter, ornate cabinets filled with old jars and a large brass chandelier.

256 LE CHAPEAU D'OR

Rue Souverain
Pont 36
Liège
+32 (0)477 98 62 92
lechapeaudor.be

Virginie Ancion can be spotted most days working on a new hat in her cluttered Liège workshop. She creates fabulous designs for women and men using old techniques and displays them in a beautiful corner shop. She will also restore a dusty old hat you have come across in your grandmother's attic.

257 DROGISTERIJ DE WALVIS

Ankerstraat 27
Sint-Niklaas
East Flanders

The interior of this beautiful old drugstore in Sint-Niklaas has barely changed since it opened in the summer of 1919. The distinctive red-fronted shop closed in 2007 but everything has been preserved intact, including the window displays and the rows of green drawers inside the shop. You can even see ancient adverts slowly peeling off the wall inside the door.

257 DROGISTERIJ DE WALVIS

Inspiring **BOOKSTORES**

258 THEORIA

Casinoplein 10
Kortrijk
West Flanders
+32 (0)56 21 62 17
theoria.be

You will find one of the most beautiful bookshops in Europe on a quiet square in Kortrijk. It occupies a grand neoclassical building that had been occupied over the years by a casino, concert hall, school and bank. Lovingly restored in 2017, the building is now home to a spectacular bookshop with a grand entrance hall, polished parquet floors

258 **THEORIA**

and a sweeping marble staircase. The owners have added interesting details, like life-size figures from Tintin comics, photographs of visiting writers and a striking landscape in the hall by the artist and filmmaker Klaus Verscheure. The book selection includes serious fiction, photography books, travel guides and kids' literature. Theoria also organises readings, cookery sessions and even piano lessons. And there are armchairs and little tables scattered around where you can sit with an espresso coffee or a local beer.

259 BARBÓÉK

Schrijnmakers-
straat 17
Leuven
Flemish Brabant
+32 (0)16 58 03 68
barboek.be

This beautiful bookshop is hidden down a quiet cobbled lane in the centre of Leuven. Located in a former printing works, it displays books in several intimate rooms furnished with round tables, armchairs and sofas. You can sit among the books with a coffee or outside in the little courtyard when the weather is fine.

260 STAD LEEST

Oudaan 18
Antwerp
+32 (0)3 233 08 80
stadleest.be

Wouter Cajot believes passionately in books and writing. He opened his spacious bookshop in 2011 in a beautiful Antwerp townhouse and moved in 2020 to a larger space where he has added a coffee bar serving lunch. The store stocks a wide range of art and lifestyle books, kids' reading and contemporary fiction, including a generous selection of books in English. You can also pick up vinyl records, postcards and stationery.

261 FILIGRANES

Avenue des
Arts 39-42
Etterbeek
Brussels
+32 (0)2 511 90 15
filigranes.be

Founded in Brussels by Marc Filipson, Filigranes has evolved into one of the world's largest bookshops. The sprawling store has sections dedicated to French fiction, art, travel and international magazines, along with English and Dutch books and even a wine corner. Open every day, it has a bright literary cafe at the back where you can start the day with coffee and croissant.

262 COOK & BOOK

Place du
Temps Libre 1
Woluwe-Saint-
Lambert
Brussels
+32 (0)2 761 26 00
cookandbook.com

Here is one of our favourite spots in Belgium. Located in a quiet Brussels suburb, Cook & Book is one of the world's most astonishing bookshops. It occupies a row of nine shops built around a modern amphitheatre. Designed by interior architects Delacroix & Friant, the colourful, quirky interiors are dedicated to themes like travel, literature, comics and cookbooks. But there are also themed dining areas, a cafe and even a jazz bar. You can book a table for five inside a shiny American Airstream caravan, meet for lunch in an Italian trattoria or sit down to dinner in a retro Parisian bistro. It is an inspiring, slightly baffling place, open every day from early morning until after dark. Located next to Rodebeek metro station.

263 PAARD VAN TROJE

Kouter 113
Ghent
East Flanders
+32 (0)9 330 08 83
paardvantroje.be

The independent Ghent bookshop Paard van Troje (Wooden Horse of Troy) attracts literature fans from all over the Low Countries. They come here for the eclectic range of titles, the relaxed atmosphere and the friendly staff.

264 DE ZONDVLOED

Onze-Lieve-
Vrouwestraat 70
Mechelen
Antwerp
+32 (0)15 64 03 79
dezondvloed.be

De Zondvloed (The Flood) occupies three floors of a former art deco theatre in the heart of Mechelen. The sprawling space is filled with novels, magazines and artist's books. Most of the stock is in Dutch, but they have interesting new English fiction on a table at the front. Three floors up, you find a cafe where you can sit at the window looking down on the street life.

265 CRONOPIO

Kasteelplein-
straat 21
Antwerp
+32 (0)3 226 68 94
cronopio.be

This beautiful little bookshop and coffee bar occupies a modernist building in Antwerp's Zuid district. The interior has a sober Nordic feel with pale wood shelves, colourful cafe furniture and a tiny children's den at the back. The owner offers a small, well-chosen selection of titles in Dutch, English and Spanish, along with copies of the *New York Review of Books* to browse through in the coffee bar.

264 **DE ZONDVLOED**

Creative CONCEPT STORES

266 CIMORNÉ

Alfred Nichelsstraat 14
Aalst
East Flanders
cimorne.be

An abandoned mirror factory on the edge of Aalst has been turned into a creative hub for local entrepreneurs. The striking 1920s industrial interior has been taken over by several small businesses including a bike store, a hipster barber and a plant shop with greenery hanging from an old canoe. But the most striking feature is a wooden indoor bike course. The space is lit by circular lamps made from bicycle wheels hung from the roof and the walls (even in the toilets) are covered with nostalgic photographs of Belgian cycling heroes. You can drop in for a coffee and maybe hit a day with a plant workshop or a concert on the programme.

267 PELOTON DE PARIS

Bruul 106
Mechelen
Antwerp
+32 (0)15 64 48 26
pelotondeparis.cc

Two bike fans quit their corporate jobs in 2013 to create a concept store and urban hangout dedicated to cycling. They sell cool lycra jerseys and a range of cycling accessories in their store in the heart of Mechelen. They also show bike races on a TV screen, serve good coffee, and organise local rides out of town.

268 LULU KANAL

Quai des Charbonnages 78-80
Brussels
+32 (0)2 673 09 77
luluhomeinterior.be

The Brussels concept store LuLu opened a second branch next to the canal in the summer of 2020. The spacious store on two floors occupies an 1896 art nouveau building designed by Victor Horta. Originally a cooperative bakery run by the Maison du Peuple, the industrial building is now filled with contemporary Nordic furniture, design objects and art. There's also a friendly cafe that offers coffee, homemade lunches and beers from small local breweries.

269 MY EX BOYFRIEND

Onze-Lieve-Vrouwestraat 106
Mechelen
Antwerp
myexboyfriend.info

It started out as a pop-up, but My Ex Boyfriend has now established a permanent store in Mechelen. The young owners sell an assortment of vintage desks and cabinets, along with cards, books, bags and gadgets. They also provide some helpful hints on interior design.

270 ST. VINCENTS

Kleine Markt 13
Antwerp
+32 (0)492 31 41 59
stvincents.co

Henri and Geraldine transformed a vast abandoned printing workshop in the heart of Antwerp into an original concept store. They have kept the rugged industrial look, the old guillotine table and a row of antique electricity meters, but added hanging plants, wood cabinets and a coffee bar. The store stocks a handpicked range of clothes, bags, ceramic objects and skincare products.
A little side room displays handmade baskets and towels by YuYu of Amsterdam, while another intimate space is given over to fragile fabrics by Japanese designers.

271 GOÛTS ET COULEURS

Ezelstraat 1 and 5
Bruges
West Flanders
+32 (0)50 69 82 83
gouts-et-couleurs.be

Interior designer Ester De Vestele has two small shops in Bruges dedicated to Nordic design. One shop focuses on the latest trends in chairs, tables, lamps and vases by brands such as Hay, Ferm Living and Muuto. The other shop two doors down sells affordable accessories including candles, jewellery and cards.

272 THE OTHER SHOP

Mageleinstraat 40
Ghent
East Flanders
+32 (0)9 328 00 82

Melkmarkt 31
Antwerp
+32 (0)3 225 31 72
theothershop.be

With branches in Ghent and Antwerp, The Other Shop sells an inspiring range of art books, cards and novels. The shop interiors are decorated in a bright, Nordic style with bare brick walls and large windows. The perfect spots to search for a gift for a friend, or something to read on holiday.

273 PERRON 47

Stationsstraat 47
Sint-Niklaas
East Flanders
+32 (0)3 777 00 47
perron47.com

This spacious concept store on Sint-Niklaas' stylish Stationsstraat started out as a little pop-up. You find Serax glassware, Jansen cups and gadgets that might make a fun gift. The store also has some books, original paintings and modern sculpture out in the back garden.

274 **URBAN THERAPY**

Rue de Flandre 84
Brussels
+32 (0)2 319 44 42
urbantherapy.store

Rue Blaes 96-B
Brussels

Anis and Céline have created a stunning concept store where local creatives are encouraged to realise their ideas. The inspiring interior has a relaxed jungle look with more than 50 miniature terrariums filled with exotic plants. The store also sells clothes, books, bags and jewellery by small brands. The owners offer a programme of weekend brunches accompanied by opera singers, along with terrarium workshops and DIY sessions. Plus a free cup of herbal tea while you wander around the shop. In 2020 they opened a second and equally wonderful store at Rue Blaes 96-B.

275 **HENRIETTE & JULIETTE**

Broodstraat 25
Oudenaarde
East Flanders
+32 (0)477 25 32 55
henriette-juliette.be

A beautiful store filled with trendy furniture, jewellery by Wouters & Hendrix and fashionable house plants. The owners also have a small delicatessen corner where you can gather some supplies for a dinner party, like a bottle of Strange Donkey winter gin from Antwerp, a pack of Italian pasta or a litre of organic olive oil.

276 THELMA COFFEE & DESIGN

Vaartstraat 12
Leuven
Flemish Brabant
+32 (0)471 09 97 46
thelmacoffee design.com

This beautiful white store occupies an impressive art deco interior in Leuven. The owner, who was a dentist in a previous life, named her store after her daughter. She sells minimalist Nordic furniture, stylish kids' clothes from Copenhagen and cool design objects. There's a bright coffee bar in the store where you can sit down with a flat white and flick through a design magazine.

277 PIET MOODSHOP

Sint-Pietersnieuw-straat 94
Ghent
East Flanders
+32 (0)9 278 69 78
pietmoodshop.be

Graanmarkt 2
Antwerp
+32 (0)3 500 04 00

Christoph Verbeke opened his first design store in 2012 in a former pharmacy near Ghent university. He has kept the old wood interior and tiled floor as a backdrop for an inspiring collection of pens, fashion accessories, plants and books. In 2018 he opened a second and equally tempting store in Ghent (Hippoliet Lippensplein 22), where the focus is more on office supplies, notebooks and quirky gadgets. In 2020 PIET Moodshop came to Antwerp: this third shop, in a monumental building on one of the city's most beautiful squares, is more about interior, from decorative accessories to larger pieces of furniture, by different inspiring brands, including the work of local designers. The space is truly stunning and also houses the apero bar and restaurant Grandeux.

276 THELMA COFFEE & DESIGN

LA MANUFACTURE URBAINE

FOOD

Uncommon EATING

278 LA BUVETTE

Chaussée d'Alsemberg 108
Saint-Gilles
Brussels
+32 (0)2 534 13 03
la-buvette.be

This little Brussels bistro is one of the most exciting spots to eat in Brussels. It occupies a former butcher's shop with a vintage art deco interior. The ground floor still has the original polished wood, tiled walls and menacing steel meat hooks hanging from the ceiling.
The young French chef Nicolas Scheidt works here to create a five-course set menu that changes according to the seasons. His adventurous cooking style has hints of Japan as well as the Alsace region where he was born. And the organic bread comes from his own bakery Hopla Geiss on the other side of the street.

279 GAARKEUKEN 110

Vosseschijn-straat 21
Antwerp
+32 (0)3 541 00 30
gaarkeuken110.be

There's nothing fancy about Gaarkeuken 110. It's an old harbour workers' restaurant located in a desolate area of the docks next to stacks of shipping containers. It has been serving basic Flemish food and decent beer for more than a century. You sit at a simple wooden table with your bowl of soup and listen to the babble of voices all around. Open from 5 am until 8 pm.

280 FONG MEI

Van Arteveldestraat 65-67
Antwerp
+32 (0)3 225 06 54
fongmei.be

This little restaurant in the heart of Antwerp's Chinatown doesn't look too promising. It has old furniture, paper tablecloths, stacks of wine boxes left lying around and a poster of Hong Kong at night. But don't be put off. This is the real thing, full of noisy Chinese people who work in the neighbourhood. You are handed a menu with a long list of specialities, including 34 dim sum dishes made by a dedicated dim sum chef who learned his craft in Hong Kong. Some wonderful sensations are produced, like steamed shrimp balls with crab, and steamed pork and shrimp dumpling. You won't be disappointed.

281 IL CARDINALE

Sint-Rombouts Kerkhof 1
Mechelen
Antwerp
+32 (0)468 21 00 91
ilcardinale.be

Two young graphic designers have created a hip hamburger restaurant across the road from Mechelen Cathedral. The bright interior is decorated with raw concrete walls, wood floors and bare lamps. The cheeky pair have added a touch of heresy by decorating one wall with statues of the Virgin and giving their burgers names like Holy Guacamole, Mary Had a Little Lamb and Noah and the Fish. Their final wicked touch is to play loud Gregorian chants in the basement toilets. Heaven help us.

282 LA MANUFACTURE URBAINE

Rue de Brabant 2
Charleroi
Hainaut
+32 (0)71 30 60 13
manufacture-urbaine.com

It's worth hunting out this exciting new space hidden down a quiet side street near Charleroi Sud station. Known as La Manufacture Urbaine, or more simply LaM-U, it opened in 2017 in an impressive former printing house on four floors with white concrete beams, exposed brick and industrial fittings. The vast airy space incorporates a microbrewery producing six different beers, a bakery and a coffee-roasting corner. They serve food from small farms in the Charleroi region, including Colombus pork from Marcel Biron et Fils. Photo exhibitions and indie concerts also take place in this buzzing spot.

282 LA MANUFACTURE URBAINE

283 **DE RUYFFELAER**

Gustave De Stuersstraat 11
Ypres
West Flanders
+32 (0)499 41 51 98
deruyffelaer.be

Formerly known as the Café de la Tour (the old name is still visible), De Ruyffelaer is a warm, welcoming Flemish restaurant decorated with wood panelling, brick walls and antique tools. The kitchen produces typical regional cooking such as wild boar pâté and rabbit simmered in beer with bacon and raisins, while beers include the house ale Oud Yper. An open fire is lit in winter to add to the romantic mood.

284 **BED VAN NAPOLEON**

Kortrijkstraat 101
Linden
Flemish Brabant
+32 (0)16 62 07 04
bedvannapoleon.be

This old Flemish restaurant is located in an isolated spot in the Linden woods near Leuven. It occupies an old farmhouse where Napoleon apparently sheltered from a storm in 1810. The owners have created a warm interior with antiques, candles and a blazing log fire. They offer a menu dedicated to Flemish specialities along with local ales from Lupus Brewery.

285 **LA GRANDE POSTE**

Quai sur Meuse 19
Liège
lagrandeposte.be

Abandoned for 20 years, the main post office in the heart of Liège was finally restored in 2021. The beautiful neo-Gothic building on the Meuse waterfront has reopened as a co-working space, with a food hall and craft brewery on the ground floor. You can pick up street food at one of seven stands and drink a beer on the rooftop terrace. Open every day.

Inspiring LUNCH SPOTS

286 **IN DE ZON**
Dikkebusstraat 80
De Klijte
West Flanders
+32 (0)57 21 26 26
indezon.be

This is a charming Flemish country inn filled with antiques, old photographs and cycling memorabilia. It stands on a hill with a terrace that looks out across the rolling hills of Heuvelland. The owner Dirk is a former Belgian cyclist who with his wife Cathy has created a convivial place to enjoy traditional Flemish food accompanied by a local beer.

287 **MA FERME EN VILLE**
Rue Souverain Pont 34
Liège
+32 (0)4 222 16 60
mafermeenville.be

Hidden down a narrow cobbled lane in the heart of Liège, Ma Ferme en Ville is a bright, friendly place with colourful tables, vintage crockery and moody French chanson in the background. Owner Marie Doutrepont sells local products from the Ardennes including beers from Brasserie Bellevaux in Malmédy and jars of mustard.

288 **FERNAND OBB DELICATESSEN**
Rue de Tamines 27
Saint-Gilles
Brussels
+32 (0)2 771 91 08
fernand-obb.be

The young chef Cédric Mosbeux has launched a modern New York style deli in a quiet Saint-Gilles street. The name comes from his cat Fernand and the mediaeval place name Obbrussel. His loyal customers squeeze inside to eat delicious *croquettes de crevettes* (shrimp croquettes), sandwiches with home-smoked Scotch salmon, and pastrami sandwiches served with pickles and Tierenteyn mustard from Ghent.

289 DE PEERDE-VISSCHER

Pastoor Schmitz-straat 4
Oostduinkerke
West Flanders
+32 (0)58 51 32 57

The reconstructed 1920s Flemish tavern next to the fishing museum in Oostduinkerke serves some of the best seafood on the coast. The interior has a rustic look with red-and-white checked tablecloths and odd bits of ship's equipment. The kitchen hits the right note with locals by serving stacks of fresh sole fried in butter, accompanied by big bowls of golden fries and local beers. The restaurant is run by a couple who come from a local family of shrimp fishermen, which adds to the authentic mood.

290 SANBA

Rijnkaai 22
Antwerp
+32 (0)478 32 85 05
sanba.be

This relaxed coffee and lunch spot in Antwerp's Eilandje district opened in 2017 in a brick building once owned by the Red Star Line. The carving of a United States eagle on the front dates from the time when passengers' luggage was stored here. The ground floor has been given a relaxed Nordic look by Brussels design studio Pjmares, using rough concrete, hanging plants and mirrors. The building is shared with a co-working space which ensures a lively international buzz. Drop in at lunchtime for a bowl of homemade soup or take a break from work on the terrace with a coffee and a copy of *Kinfolk* magazine.

291 DE 7 ZONDEN

Leiestraat 22
Kortrijk
West Flanders
+32 (0)56 28 09 05
d7z.be

It's easy to miss this restaurant hidden inside a government building in the centre of Kortrijk. It's a relaxed place with raw wood tables, old beer crates turned into bookcases and potted ferns. It also has a leafy courtyard where you can eat out in the sun. The people back in the kitchen create amazing dishes using fresh local ingredients. The inexpensive daily menu starts with a big tureen of homemade soup and a basket of thick brown bread, followed by a sophisticated main course such as monkfish with spinach puree, bright green samphire and *beurre blanc*.

292 STOOM

Bergstraat 5
Vilvoorde
Flemish Brabant
+32 (0)478 83 25 11
stoomvilvoorde.be

Three friends opened a striking coffee bar and lunch spot in the heart of Vilvoorde in 2020. Located in a corner building that was once a bank, it's a bright, contemporary space with big windows looking out on the street. And there's a surprise in the basement where the owners have created a kids' playroom inside the bank's vault. Locals come here for a healthy soup, or a homemade quiche, or just to meet friends for coffee.

293 LITTLE PARIS

Chaussée de
Bruxelles 89
Waterloo
Walloon Brabant
+32 (0)2 354 84 57
little-paris.be

The perfect local spot for an affordable lunch after a visit to Waterloo battlefield, this contemporary bistro offers sophisticated cooking in a relaxed setting. French chef Arold Bourgeois has built up a solid reputation with his flamboyant dishes featuring ingredients sourced from hand-picked suppliers in Belgium and France. But be sure to book ahead.

294 BOULE DE BLEU

R. de la Coupe 46
Mons
Hainaut
+32 (0)65 84 58 19
bouledebleu.com

A rambling, bohemian place in Mons with wooden floors, ancient objects hung from the roof beams and toilets like mini art galleries. The young, multilingual staff are irresistibly charming as they serve generous salads with unexpected ingredients like Belgian *boudin blanc* (white sausage).

295 CULTUURCAFÉ

Hendrik Serruyslaan 18-A
Ostend
West Flanders
+32 (0)496 25 84 88
degrotepost.be

This bustling cafe is located in the monumental Grote Post building in the heart of Ostend. Renovated in 2012, the interior has kept the modernist looks of this former post office including huge windows, etched glass panels and a row of 12 telephone booths (now framing large portraits of modern Flemish writers and musicians). The kitchen offers a plain modern menu based on local organic products.

Classic BELGIAN FOOD

296 MUSSELS
OESTERPUT
Wenduinse-steenweg 16
Blankenberge
West Flanders
+32 (0)50 41 10 35
oesterput.com

No booking. Nothing fancy. Just perfect seafood. The Devriendt family runs a huge wooden restaurant on the Blankenberge quayside that resembles a New England clam shack. It is very basic, but they serve some of the best seafood on the coast, including dripping wet oysters, little whelks extracted from their shell with a pin and lobsters kept in large bubbling tanks.

297 STOOFVLEES
NÜETNIGENOUGH
Rue du Lombard 25
Brussels
nuetnigenough.be

Stoofvlees, or *Carbonades à la Flamande*, is the ultimate Belgian comfort food. This thick Flemish beef stew is slowly simmered in dark Belgian beer to create a rich, sweet flavour. It is normally brought to your table in a small iron casserole pot, along with a side serving of proper Belgian fries. You can find stoofvlees (sometimes called *stoverij*) in most traditional Belgian brasseries such as Nüetnigenough in the heart of Brussels.

298 ZWEZERIK
CIRO'S
Amerikalei 6
Antwerp
+32 (0)3 238 11 47
ciros.be

Ciro's is a classic Belgian restaurant dating from 1962. The wood-panelled interior has hardly changed since it opened and the menu lists old Belgian favourites, like the mysterious *zwezerik* (lamb or veal sweetbread). But you can also order Irish rib steak served with pepper sauce and a portion of frites.

298 **ZWEZERIK**

299 SHRIMP CROQUETTES

LES BRASSERIES GEORGES

Avenue Winston Churchill 259
Uccle
Brussels
+32 (0)2 347 21 00
brasseriesgeorges.be

The *croquette de crevette*, or *garnaalkroket*, is a classic Belgian dish. It is composed of a crispy croquette filled with tiny North Sea shrimps cooked in a creamy sauce. In the best restaurants, the croquettes are served with deep-fried parsley and a slice of lemon. Head to the lively Les Brasseries Georges on the edge of the Brussels woods to try their excellent version.

300 LIÈGE WAFFLES

UNE GAUFRETTE SAPERLIPOPETTE
Rue des Mineurs 7
Liège
+32 (0)4 222 37 13
une-gaufrette-saperlipopette.be

The name is tricky for foreigners to say, but Une Gaufrette Saperlipopette is the place to go for a sticky Liège waffle. Eric Michaux faithfully follows a traditional recipe to make fluffy waffles using the best butter, eggs and sugar. He sells them in a tiny shop around the corner from the lively Place du Marché. You may have to queue outside for a while because word is getting around that these are possibly the best waffles in the land.

301 TOMATES CREVETTES

BRASSERIE BRISTOL
Zeedijk 291
Knokke-Heist
West Flanders
+32 (0)50 51 21 12
brasseriebristol.be

Brasserie Bristol stands on the Heist seafront on the site of the grand Bristol Hotel. Established in 1927, it offers those simple, classic dishes Belgians like to eat at the coast, such as tomatoes filled with grey shrimps. But the kitchen can do more sophisticated dishes as well. It's worth phoning to book a table by the window to enjoy the sea view.

302 BOULETS LIÉGOIS

LES TERRASSES
Avenue Rogier 1
Liège
+32 (0)498 36 66 77
lesterrasses-liege.com

The friendly local brasserie Les Terrasses is one of the best spots in Liège to sample the local speciality *Boulets Liégois*. It occupies a handsome corner building lit with red neon signs in the heart of the old town. The Liège speciality involves large meatballs cooked in a rich, dark sauce flavoured with sweet *Sirop de Liège*, fried onions, prunes and a sprig of parsley. Served with fries and a glass of Belgian beer, it is the perfect winter dish. Some restaurant menus mysteriously list the dish as *Boulets sauce Lapin*, or meatballs in rabbit sauce, although no chef has ever cooked it with rabbit.

303 POTJEVLEESCH

DE BARBIER
Hillestraat 5
Heuvelland
West Flanders
+32 (0)57 44 59 24

You come across the traditional dish *Potjevleesch* (potted meat) in small inns in West Flanders close to the French border. The wood-panelled De Barbier in Dranouter is one of the best places to try this local dish made with chicken, rabbit and veal preserved in jelly. Local people love it, served with a bowl of frites and a beer.

304 MAZERINETAART

BAKKERIJ VANDECASTEELE
Ieperstraat 47
Poperinge
West Flanders
+32 (0)57 33 32 89
bakkerijvandecasteele.be

The sweet sponge cake Mazerinetaart is a Poperinge speciality sold in local bakeries and served in some restaurants. It takes its name from Cardinal Jules Mazarin who invented the recipe in 1885 by soaking sponge cake in warm butter and cinnamon sauce. The result is a sweet, sticky pudding that goes well with a strong coffee.

305 ICE CREAM

CREMERIE FRANÇOIS
Ankerstraat 34
Sint-Niklaas
East Flanders
+32 (0)3 776 10 50
cremerie-francois.com

Locals have been treating themselves to ice-cream sundaes in Cremerie François since it opened in Sint-Niklaas in 1928. Located near the main square, it's now a spacious modern salon with neon lights and enlarged old photographs taken in the streets of Sint-Niklaas in the 1920s. They make their own creamy ice cream from local milk following a secret recipe.

Small CHOCOLATE SHOPS

306 **CHOCOLATIER M**
Sylvain Dupuisstraat 38
Knokke-Heist
West Flanders
+32 (0)50 61 44 60
chocolatier-m.be

David Maenhout creates tiny chocolates in a workshop behind his shop in Knokke using the finest Belgian chocolate. He comes up with endless creative ideas for combining different flavours like gin and tonic, mango with balsamic vinegar, and lemon with coriander seeds. But not just any lemon. It has to be exclusive Calamansi lemon from South East Asia.

307 **DEFROIDMONT**
Briscol 19-A
Érezée
Luxembourg
+32 (0)86 21 84 40
chocolaterie-defroidmont.be

Philippe Defroidmont picked a remote spot deep in the Ardennes to establish his chocolate workshop. For more than 35 years, he has made unique chocolates in small batches using unexpected ingredients. You can watch the team at work through a large window and find out more about the business in a small family museum.

308 V-CHOCOLATIER BY SWEERTVAEGHER

Geldmuntstraat 39
Bruges
West Flanders
+32 (0)471 85 30 73
v-chocolatier.be

The Sweertvaegher family opened their first chocolate shop in Ypres in 1933 and expanded to Kortrijk in 1946 and Bruges in 1950. Now rebranded V-chocolatier, they have relocated to a chic little store furnished with a vintage wooden counter that once stood in their Kortrijk store. Locals come here to buy handmade praline chocolates with chic names like Grenoble and Snobinette.

308 V-CHOCOLATIER BY SWEERTVAEGHER

309 BOON

Paardsdemer-straat 13
Hasselt
Limburg
+32 (0)11 42 21 99
chocolade huisboon.be

Patrick Mertens and Inge Lijnen recently opened a beautiful chocolate shop in a grand Hasselt town house. Mertens makes the chocolates in an open workshop where you can watch him stir in unusual flavours like juniper, summer fruits and smoke-dried Mexican pepper. You can sit in the romantic salon with a coffee and two handmade chocolates or pick up an elegant hand-wrapped box to take home.

310 CHOCOLATERIE LEDOUX

Boezingestraat 133
Langemark
West Flanders
+32 (0)57 48 92 22
choc-ledoux.be

Located on the road from Ypres to Langemark, this is not the easiest place to find. Founded in the 1970s, it is now run by a young couple who make authentic chocolates in a workshop next to the shop. They specialise in seashells which they make by hand in special moulds.

Roadside FRIES STANDS

311 AU P'TIT CREUX

Route de Marche 9
Baillonville
Namur
+32 (0)84 32 22 59
aupetitcreux-baillonville.be

The *friterie* Au P'tit Creux occupies a long white cabin next to a busy road in the Ardennes. You order frites at the window and sit inside at a plain Formica table. There's nothing fancy here, except maybe the checked curtains. It might look basic, but it's a warm, welcoming spot in the harsh Ardennes landscape.

312 DE BLAUWE FRITUUR

Doornikse-steenweg 22
Kortrijk
West Flanders
+32 (0)56 25 20 04
deblauwefrituur.be

The blue façade marks out this friendly fries shop in the heart of Kortrijk's student district. The owner and his daughter create perfect Belgian fries using local Bintje potatoes. They also prepare a rich *stoofvlees* (stew) simmered in Bellegems Bruin beer. Locals claim it is the best *frituur* in Kortrijk.

313 FRITERIE MARSUPILAMI

Route de Marche
Bastogne
Luxembourg

The busy N4 highway used to have dozens of roadside frites stands where tourists and truck drivers would pull off the road on the long drive through the Ardennes. Many have closed down, but Friterie Marsupilami has survived. It occupies an old yellow bus parked next to the road outside Bastogne. Named after an invented animal in a Belgian comic strip, it's a friendly spot to wait in line while the fries are prepared.

314 'T KASTAARKE

314 'T KASTAARKE

Kustlaan 102
Zeebrugge
West Flanders
+32 (0)50 54 54 75

This smart modern frites shop near Zeebrugge church looks like a roadside diner. Everyone comes here, from dock workers in oily overalls to elderly couples who have retired to the coast. As well as excellent frites, you can order a bowl of fish soup or fried North Sea sole.

315 'T KANON

Wulvestraat 55
Zillebeke
West Flanders
+32 (0)57 20 54 21

This is a smart modern roadside frites shop on the route from Ypres to Zillebeke. It's popular with locals as well as Dutch tourists on the war trail. The owner fries each batch separately using the best potatoes.

LE CIRIO

DRINKS

Authentic BELGIAN CAFES

316 **IN DE VERZEKERING TEGEN DE GROTE DORST**

Frans Baetens-straat 45
Eizeringen, near Lennik
Flemish Brabant
+32 (0)2 532 58 58
dorst.be

No one could really believe it in 2016 when In de Verzekering Tegen de Grote Dorst (Insurance against a Huge Thirst) was voted the best bar in the world. It is after all just a rustic local cafe next to the church in a Flemish village near Brussels. And it is only open for ten hours every week – on Sundays, holidays and after local funerals. But the website RateBeer has put it at the top of their ranking. Run by two brothers and their mother, the cafe stocks hundreds of Lambic beers produced in the local area, including some very rare bottles. The owners believe their bar became famous after a group of beer tourists ended up there after their bus got lost in the rolling hills. It has a rather austere 1950s interior, no food and no credit card machine, but it is truly authentic, with a mix of locals and beer enthusiasts creating a relaxed mood.

317 **DE KAT**

Wolstraat 22
Antwerp
+32 (0)3 233 08 92

De Kat is one of those old Antwerp bars where nothing much has changed in a hundred years. It still has the original wood panelling, mirrors and tiled floor. This is the perfect place to taste the local De Koninck beer served in a round glass known as a *bolleke*.

318 LEUVEN CENTRAL

Margarethaplein 3
Leuven
Flemish Brabant
+32 (0)16 20 81 27

This genuine Leuven *volkscafé* opened in 2015 in an abandoned corner cafe, near a plaque to mark the official centre of Leuven. The new owners have carefully preserved the original interior with its wooden furniture, Stella Artois signs and rows of aspidistras on the window sills. They offer authentic Flemish bar food, like *pistolets met hesp* (ham rolls), homemade meat balls and even a basket of hard boiled eggs on the counter.

318 LEUVEN CENTRAAL

319 POSTHOTEL

Stationsplein 11
Wetteren
East Flanders
+32 (0)477 39 77 45
cafeposthotel.be

The hotel closed a long time ago, but the cafe opposite the station in Wetteren is still called the Posthotel. Built in 1887, it was originally a coaching inn on the road from Antwerp to Ghent. The bar is decorated in Flemish Renaissance style with carved wood panelling, paintings of drinking scenes in the style of Pieter Bruegel and Flemish proverbs in neat gilt letters. Open from Friday to Sunday.

320 LE CIRIO

Rue de la Bourse 18
Brussels
+32 (0)2 512 13 95
lecirio.be

This gorgeous cafe started out in 1886 as a delicatessen selling Italian specialities. It was founded by Francesco Cirio from Turin, who made his fortune selling tinned tomatoes. He opened similar establishments in 18 cities across Europe, but this cafe in Brussels is the only one to survive. The interior was redesigned by Henri Coosemans in 1909 in the style of an Italian grand café. It still has the original carved wooden bar, gleaming iron chandelier and old signs advertising Cinzano.

320 LE CIRIO

321 LA FLEUR EN PAPIER DORÉ

Rue des Alexiens 53-55
Brussels
+32 (0)2 511 16 59
goudblommeke inpapier.be

How can anyone resist a bar called The Flower in Gold Paper? Originally called the Café des Artistes, it acquired its more romantic name after it was taken over in 1944 by the eccentric poet Geert Van Bruaene. It became a popular meeting place for a distinctly odd group of Belgian artists and writers including René Magritte. It still has its old iron stove, tiled floor and ageing wooden furniture. The three dark little rooms are crammed with old objects that don't belong together, including faded newspaper cuttings, strange oil paintings and a dusty South African parrot.

322 BRASSERIE DU PARC

Marie-Joséplein 3
Ostend
West Flanders
+32 (0)59 70 16 80
hotelduparc.be

Brasserie du Parc has hardly changed since it opened in 1928. The old leather sofas, brass coat hooks, large mirrors and tiled toilets are all still there. Along with the retired couples living comfortably on their pensions and the formal waiters in black aprons. The filter coffee dribbles into a glass cup. It is slow, but then no one is in much of a hurry here.

323 CAFÉ VLISSINGHE

Blekersstraat 2
Bruges
West Flanders
+32 (0)50 34 37 37
cafevlissinghe.be

Founded in 1515, this is the oldest tavern in Bruges. It still has most of its original furnishings, including a wooden counter carved in the 16th century, an iron stove and a chair possibly owned by the Flemish artist Anthony Van Dyck. It's best to come here in winter when the old iron stove is burning and the locals are hunched over their Trappist beers.

324 Ô'S ARCADES

Rue Jean Bertholet 4
Vielsalm
Luxembourg
+32 (0)499 25 17 74
osarcades.be

Some Ardennes cafes can seem quite austere. Not this place opposite the church in Vielsalm. It's a cheerful spot decorated in the style of an Ardennes farmhouse with old photographs, religious relics and ancient shop scales. The cafe brews its own house beer called Ô'Poil, which is only sold on the spot. The owner also serves good coffee and traditional hot chocolate, as well as traditional Belgian food.

Unusual BARS

325 **SAS 6**
Jaagpad along Kanaal Herentals-Bochold, Sas VI
Mol
Antwerp
+32 (0)14 31 11 40
sas6.be

It's not easy to find Sas 6. You might need to talk to a local. This idyllic waterfront cafe is located at Lock 6 on the canal near Mol. The authentic Flemish interior has two dark rooms furnished with antique lamps, oil paintings and red velvet cinema seats. There are tables out in the garden under the lime trees where cyclists stop off for an Oude Geuze beer and a bowl of soup. It is possibly the most romantic bar in Belgium, even if it is one of the hardest to find.

326 **BUVETTE SINT-SEBASTIAAN**
PARC JOSAPHAT
Avenue Ambassadeur Van Vollenhoven
Schaerbeek
Brussels
buvettesintsebastiaan.com

You might easily miss it as you wander through the romantic Parc Josaphat, past artificial waterfalls and strange bronze statues. The *buvette* is a plain brick building with rustic wood details near the mini golf course. For many years, it was a private clubhouse where the guild of archers met for beer and dry sausage after practising on the archery range. But it was renovated in 2015 by one of the founders of the Brasserie de la Senne. He turned it into a little bar in the park where you can go for a beer and some simple food. But he also came up with creative ideas to bring people to this hidden spot, like summer jazz concerts, beer tastings and a Friday fish party with rare varieties on the menu.

327 CAFÉ BERTRAND

Rue M. Nisen 16
Ster,
Francorchamps
Liège
+32 (0)475 27 62 17

The owners of this authentic Ardennes village store and cafe go out of their way to create a friendly atmosphere. You can drop in for a packet of pasta, perch on a bar stool with a local beer or sit down at one of the wooden tables for a plate of Liège meatballs. The cafe is packed with racing fans any time the Grand Prix is held in Francorchamps.

328 HUYZE BEGGA

Begijnhof 31
Kortrijk
West Flanders
+32 (0)498 76 16 24
huyzebegga.be

A step-gabled house inside the walls of Kortrijk's Begijnhof is now occupied by a coffee house. Formerly the home of the Mother Superior, the 17th-century building was beautifully restored in 2016. It is a relaxed, modern place where you can order coffee, tea or a local beer. The little garden at the front has a few small tables where you can sit in the sun listening to the church bells.

329 LE CAPPUCCINO 1971

Rue des Croisiers 40
Liège
+32 (0)4 252 02 62
le-cappuccino-1971.eatbu.com

A strange cafe is buried inside a curious round library in the centre of Liège. Designed by Pierre Schuster in 1971, it is a dark, mysterious den with exposed brickwork, wooden rafters and dim lighting. Furnished with old armchairs, piles of magazines and round tables, the cafe has a serious, literary atmosphere. It might look a bit odd, but the young owners have created a relaxed mood with good music, photo exhibitions and excellent espresso coffee.

327 **CAFÉ BERTRAND**

Unique COFFEE BARS

330 MAISON JACOBS
Rue Grande 147
Dinant
Namur
+32 (0)82 22 21 39

Nothing has changed in this Dinant tea room since the interior was modernised in 1948. It has kept its dark wood panelled walls, mirrors and folding tables. The coffee is still served in silver pots and the *Couques de Dinant* are made according to a recipe dating from 1860.

331 'T OUD SASHUIS
Hellestraat 20
Astene
East Flanders
+32 (0)476 81 01 14
astene-sas.be

It might be open. It might not. This is definitely one of the strangest cafes in Belgium. It occupies an old lock-keepers' house in a beautiful location on the River Leie. The dark interior is filled with a bizarre collection of maritime objects, including horns, maps and lamps. It could almost be a museum, apart from the dried sausages hanging from the rafters and the Edith Piaf record playing in the background. It's a friendly place popular with cyclists out on a Sunday morning ride and locals walking along the river bank. But it's quite primitive. The men's toilet out in the back yard is nothing more than a simple length of old drainpipe fixed to the wall.

332 KAFFEE INE
Onze-Lieve-
Vrouwestraat 6
Mechelen
Antwerp
+32 (0)475 48 58 14
kaffee-ine.com

This bohemian coffee bar in downtown Mechelen is a favourite dive for young local creatives. The cluttered interior has a shabby chic look with assorted leather armchairs, a wall plastered with photos of cycling heroes and a romantic den on the mezzanine level. Look out for concerts by indie bands.

333 CAFÉ ENTREPOT

333 CAFÉ ENTREPOT

Vaartkom 4
Leuven
Flemish Brabant
+32 (0)16 22 27 41
cafeentrepot.be

This stunning cafe opened in 2012 in a renovated industrial building on Leuven's Vaartkom waterfront. It has a rough industrial interior with recycled wooden tables, iron pipes and a suspended silver sculpture by Pieter Jansen. The terrace on the waterfront is the perfect spot for a coffee or a chilled Hoegaarden beer.

334 PHILIMONIUS

L. D'Haeseleer-straat 8
Aalst
East Flanders
+32 (0)488 20 13 58
www.philimonius.be

It's worth tracking down this friendly coffee bar hidden down a quiet lane in Aalst. Owner Jo De Bruyne has created a relaxed hipster interior with assorted vintage furniture, a window counter where you can perch with a laptop and tables out in the street. He also sells books, postcards, jewellery and unusual gifts. Locals swear the coffee served here is the best in town.

335 DE DINGEN

Budastraat 12
Kortrijk
West Flanders
+32 (0)56 90 72 57
dedingen.be

De Dingen is a quirky bar in Kortrijk furnished with odd tables, potted plants and a vintage school wall map. It's a relaxed spot with a cultural feel where they sell jewellery made by local designers and organise concerts by Kortrijk bands. They put out a few tables on the street in the summer where you can sit with a bowl of soup and a West Flanders craft beer.

336 BAR STAN

C. Meunierstraat 2
Leuven
Flemish Brabant
+32 (0)16 88 90 83
barstan.be

This is a cool neighbourhood coffee bar in Leuven's sleepy Nieuw Kwartier. The place is run by architects who designed the plywood counter and furnished the interior with old school classroom chairs, Formica tables and bare light bulbs. It's the perfect spot for a lazy Sunday brunch if you are lucky enough to secure a table.

337 CÅFÉ DU SABLØN

Rue de la
Régence 26
Brussels
+32 (0)2 503 39 99

This relaxed coffee bar in the elegant Sablon district of Brussels has embraced Nordic style right down to the letters in its name. Located in a raw concrete interior, it has perfected the Scandinavian look of pale wood, scattered cushions and international newspapers. The coffee is roasted on the spot.

Quiet TERRACES

338 UIT STEPPE & OASE
J. Breydelstraat 21
Ghent
East Flanders
+32 (0)9 224 07 36

Here is a hidden spot in the heart of Ghent where you can sit in a romantic garden at the back of an antique shop. It's a magical location with old trees, a pond and wobbly metal tables. Locals come here in the afternoon for a mint tea and a slice of cheesecake. The tiny kitchen also prepares delicate Middle Eastern food for days when you can eat outside. And if the weather is not reliable, you can sit inside in two grand Empire rooms filled with African masks and art books. Only open at weekends.

338 UIT STEPPE & OASE

339 LE JARDIN DU PESAGE

HIPPODROME DE BOITSFORT

Chaussée de la Hulpe 51-53
Uccle
Brussels
+32 (0)2 354 72 00
lejardindupesage.be

It's worth heading out of Brussels to the cafe Le Jardin du Pesage on the edge of the forest. It occupies a modernist building at the former Boitsfort racing track known as the Pesage (where jockeys were weighed before a race). Abandoned for many years, the site was finally restored by Brussels Region as a summer cafe and restaurant. Local designer Lionel Jadot was then recruited to decorate the interior in his fun, quirky style. And there are plenty of tables and deck chairs for sitting out in the sun.

340 JAM HOTEL

Chaussée de Charleroi 132
Saint-Gilles
Brussels
+32 (0)2 537 17 87
jamhotel.be

Located in the old Sint-Lucas School of Architecture, the Jam Hotel in Brussels welcomes locals and hotel guests to its rooftop bar. Take the lift to the sixth floor and you can perch on a stool next to a narrow swimming pool gazing over the roofs of Saint-Gilles. There's also a small indoor bar with a couch, bookshelves made from concrete pipes and a log fire lit on cold days.

341 MOULIN LOVERIX

Rue Werihet 25
Eben-Emael
Liège
+32 (0)4 369 28 98
loverix.be

Locals drop by for a beer on the terrace of this ancient watermill next to the pretty River Jeker. But it also attracts tourists because of its location near the historic Fort Eben-Emael and its rustic interior with tables squeezed in next to old mill machinery. The menu lists about 30 different types of pancake, along with soups, toasted sandwiches and Belgian beers.

342 COUPE MATADI

Kol. Begaultlaan 7
Leuven
Flemish Brabant
+32 (0)16 20 86 06
coupematadi.be

Once summer arrives, you can sit eating ice cream on the deck of an old Belgian river barge dating from 1929. Moored on Leuven's Vaartkom, it overlooks an interesting urban mix of modern apartments and old industrial buildings. Among the flavours, you might find some rather unusual creations like yoghurt with English lemon curd. Closed during the winter months.

343 DE GOUDEN VIS

Nauwstraat 5-7
Mechelen
Antwerp
+32 (0)15 20 72 06
degoudenvis.be

This bohemian art nouveau cafe looks a bit shabby, with bicycles parked in the hallway and faded posters peeling off the wall. But this former fishmonger's shop is a wonderful, romantic place to grab a beer. You might even, if you are lucky, find a place to sit on the little waterfront terrace shaded by an old vine.

344 'T BINNENHUYS

Gustave De Stuersstraat 8
Ypres
West Flanders
+32 (0)57 35 97 06
binnenhuys1772.be

This romantic Ypres coffee house is hidden at the back of a rambling mansion. Built in 1772, this house is one of the few buildings to survive the German artillery bombardment in the First World War. The front rooms are now occupied by an interior design store, while the cafe is hidden at the back. It takes up two small rooms furnished with old leather sofas, faded photographs and an iron stove. There is also a beautiful walled garden that catches the afternoon sun.

345 ESTAMINET IN DEN ROZENKRANS

Abdij Vlierbeek 14
Kessel-Lo
Flemish Brabant
+32 (0)16 25 63 03
in-den-rozenkrans.be

This beautiful 18th-century inn with whitewashed walls occupies the former gatehouse of Vlierbeek Abbey. The old interior has a rustic look, with heavy wood tables and old beer signs. It also has a lovely terrace shaded by old trees where local cyclists take a pause. The food is simple, but the beer list is impressive. And children can run around the courtyard.

1898 THE POST

SLEEP

Hotels in
HISTORIC HOUSES

346 GRAND HOTEL CASSELBERGH

Hoogstraat 6
Bruges
West Flanders
+32 (0)50 44 65 00
grandhotel casselbergh.be

This impressive hotel in the heart of Bruges is located in two restored buildings just a few steps from the Burg square. Named after a mediaeval palace that stood here, the hotel has spectacular 18th-century halls, old stone columns from the 15th century and a comfortable bar with a blazing fire. Some bedrooms occupy the old mansion, while others are located in a modern extension.

347 HÔTEL SÉLYS

Rue du Mont Saint-Martin 9-11
Liège
+32 (0)4 222 94 94
hotelselys.be

Located in two restored town houses, this is a gorgeous urban hotel looking down on the old town of Liège. You enter through a baroque courtyard dating from 1620, but there is an older 15th-century structure deep inside the complex. The interior design is cool, spacious and contemporary, with some striking spaces including a neoclassical ballroom, a lounge with views of the city, and a bar down in a vaulted mediaeval cellar. Somewhat confusingly, the entrance lobby is on the seventh floor, while bedrooms are on lower levels, but that's part of the charm of this ancient building.

348 THE FOURTH

Grote Markt 5
Leuven
Flemish Brabant
+32 (0)16 22 75 54
th4th.com

This stunning hotel opened in 2017 in a renovated Gothic building in the heart of Leuven. The curious name was chosen because the hotel is the fourth occupant of the building. Built in 1479 for the local guilds, it became a theatre in 1817 and a branch of the National Bank in 1930. The building has now been transformed to create a fabulous hotel where bedrooms have smart light switches and a personal supply of artisanal coffee beans from Bolivia.

348 THE FOURTH

351 **1898 THE POST**

349 RECOUR

Guido Gezelle-straat 7
Poperinge
West Flanders
+32 (0)57 33 57 25
pegasusrecour.be

This family-owned hotel occupies a former tobacco factory in Poperinge. It has a relaxed, warm feel with a spacious lounge decorated in a comfortable country house style by interior designer Pieter Porters. The eight guest rooms are furnished with big wooden beds, polished desks and retro baths, while the seven new rooms in the annex have interiors by contemporary designers.

350 THE DOMINICAN

Rue Léopold 9
Brussels
+32 (0)2 203 08 08
thedominican.be

Located in a former monastery, the Dominican is a sophisticated Brussels hotel with an interior designed by the Amsterdam firm FG stijl. It strikes a soothing note in the city centre with its airy cloister, rich fabrics and countless orchids. The hotel bar is a gorgeous place to meet friends with its high ceilings, chandeliers and comfy armchairs.

351 1898 THE POST

Graslei 16
Ghent
East Flanders
+32 (0)9 391 53 79
1898thepost.com

This striking boutique hotel opened in 2017 on the upper floors of the former central post office in Ghent. The 38 rooms are decorated in a warm style evoking the building's late 19th-century architecture, with high ceilings and antique furniture. Located in the heart of Ghent, the hotel offers its guests some of the best views in the city and has a stylish cocktail bar that could soon be the most fashionable hangout in town.

Unique **B & B S**

352 NUIT BLANCHE

Groeninge 2
Bruges
West Flanders
+32 (0)494 40 04 47
bb-nuitblanche.com

The artist David de Graef has created a fabulous guest house in a historic Bruges house he bought in 2007. The two guest rooms are designed in the style of a Jan van Eyck painting with old stone fireplaces, stained glass windows and huge oak beds. They look out on a mediaeval walled garden and a little canal, while breakfast is served in the owner's art studio.

353 VAN WASSENHOVE HOUSE

Sint-Martens-Latem
West Flanders
museumdd.be

Architecture enthusiasts can spend a weekend in a striking brutalist house designed in 1974 by the Belgian architect Juliaan Lampens. This astonishing private home in the artists' village of Sint-Martens-Latem was built of raw grey concrete, wood and glass for the Ghent teacher Albert Van Wassenhove. The house is now managed by a local art museum as a weekend B&B and artists' residence. But it's not for anyone who needs privacy. The bedroom is a simple wooden circle within the open plan design. Two bicycles are provided to explore the peaceful river landscape of the Leie.
The house can be booked for two people from May to October. Contact the Museum Dhondt-Dhaenens for details.

354 HUYZE ELIMONICA

Euphrosina Beernaertstraat 39
Ostend
West Flanders
+32 (0)479 67 07 09
elimonica.be

Filip Deschacht, a former chef, runs a sublime B&B in a fin-de-siècle town house built in 1899. He spent three years restoring the house and redecorated the rooms with rustic white furniture, contemporary paintings and maritime details like jars of seashells. The breakfast is a spectacular spread served at a long wooden table in the basement, or out in the garden if it is warm. There is even a garage across the road where you can leave your car.

355 SMOKKELMOLEN

Kleine Molenstraat 9
Kanne
Limburg
smokkelmolen.be

This stylish B&B occupies an old watermill on the River Jeker just a few metres from the Dutch border. The building was restored in 2016 to create four guest rooms, along with a library, wine cellar and waterfront terrace. The owners have carefully renovated the historic mill wheel, which is used to generate electricity and grind flour. The B&B is a short walk from the acclaimed Château Neercanne restaurant and 15 minutes by bike from Maastricht.

356 BEA B&B

Hazegrasstraat 37
Knokke
West Flanders
+32 (0)475 74 64 50
bea-bb.com

Bea Mombaers runs a sublime B&B in an old farmhouse with a thatched roof near the beach town of Knokke. You can sit out in the garden eating breakfast at a big communal table and cool off at the end of the day in the swimming pool. The three spacious guest rooms are calm, contemporary spaces with concrete floors and grey walls. Bea has furnished the rooms with an eclectic collection of 1950s vintage chairs, tables and lamps from her interior design shop, so if you like that chair in the bedroom you can just buy it on the spot.

COOL PLACES *to stay*

357 THE WOODEN HORSE

AT: LA BALADE DES GNOMES
Rowe dè Rèmoleû 20
Heyd
Luxembourg
+32 (0)472 20 86 23
labalade desgnomes.be

Nothing prepares you for a night in this eccentric hotel. Located in an isolated village in the Ardennes, it was designed by architect Dominique Noël next to his restaurant La Gargouille. Inspired by the stories of Robert Louis Stevenson and Lewis Carroll, Noël has carved out ten unique rooms incorporating endless surprising details. You can sleep in a mock forest with fish swimming in a stream, a boat floating in a pool or a gypsy caravan. But the wildest room to book is a wooden horse reached by a drawbridge with an interior on three levels. Children absolutely love spending a night here, although some might find it a bit too weird for comfort. The owners only speak French.

358 CASANUS

Westakker
Kemzeke
East Flanders
+32 (0)3 789 22 07
verbeke foundation.com

You can spend an unconventional night at the Verbeke Foundation sleeping in a giant fibreglass replica of a human intestine. Created by the artist Joep Van Lieshout, the two-room lodging stands on the edge of a lake reached across an old iron bridge. You can also sleep in Kevin Van Braak's *CampingFlats* where overnight accommodation involves one of four simple tents stacked on a metal tower, or in the new BlobVB3 designed by dmvA-architecten. An austere breakfast is served in the restaurant. But this is really the middle of nowhere. Bookings only by email.

359 **DREAM HOTEL**

Rue de la Grande
Triperie 17
Mons
Hainaut
+32 (0)65 32 97 20
hoteldream.be

A former chapel in Mons has been turned into one of the country's strangest hotels. Each of the rooms is a loving homage to Belgian icons, from the blue comic-book Smurfs to bowler-hat-obsessed Magritte. But maybe the oddest room is dedicated to Binche Carnival, with bedside tables made from drums and a carpet designed like a confetti-strewn cobbled street.

358 **CASANUS**

360 TRECK HOSTEL

Groendreef 51
Ghent
East Flanders
+32 (0)9 310 76 20
treckhostel.be

Adventurous travellers can spend the night in a vintage caravan parked inside an abandoned brickworks on the edge of Ghent. This quirky concept offers guests a room in one of nine caravans decorated in different styles, including one decorated by a Ghent street artist and another with a Hawaiian beach theme. Each caravan has its own little garden with deckchairs, random tables and potted plants. The hostel also has a bar, play area and bikes to get you into town. It's maybe not for light sleepers, but perfect for anyone looking for something a little on the wild side.

361 PAIRI DAIZA

AT: DOMAINE
DE CAMBRON
Brugelette
Hainaut
+32 (0)68 25 08 50
pairidaiza.eu

Located in the grounds of a ruined abbey, Pairi Daiza is regularly voted the best zoo in Europe. Over the years, the owner has gradually brought together a fascinating collection of endangered animals that roam in virtually wild landscapes. But the truly unique feature of this zoo is that it has guest rooms where you can spend the night next to the animals. You can pick a bedroom with a view of Siberian tigers, or a family room where your children can watch the penguins, or even an underwater room that has a view of the polar bears. The room rate is quite expensive, but includes access to the zoo and meals. Children love the experience.

INDEX

COLOPHON

EDITING *and* COMPOSING – Derek Blyth

GRAPHIC DESIGN – Joke Gossé and doublebill.design

PHOTOGRAPHY – Roel Hendrickx – www.roelh.zenfolio.com

ADDITIONAL PHOTOGRAPHY – p. 181: © VisitFlanders, photo Jan d'Hondt – p. 247: Regula Ysewijn

COVER IMAGE – Cable Car Cabin, Namur (secret 39)

The addresses in this book have been selected after thorough independent research by the author, in collaboration with Luster Publishing. The selection is solely based on personal evaluation of the business by the author. Nothing in this book was published in exchange for payment or benefits of any kind.

D/2022/12.005/9
ISBN 978 94 6058 3216
NUR 511, 510

Fourth edition, March 2022 – Seventh reprint, March 2022
lusterpublishing.com – THE500HIDDENSECRETS.COM
info@lusterpublishing.com

Printed in Italy by Printer Trento.

FSC www.fsc.org MIX Paper | Supporting responsible forestry FSC® C015829